Crowded Platforms and
Window Seats

Crowded Platforms and Window Seats

Window Seats

One Family's Interrail Adventure

Judy Yorke

First published in 2024 by The Sentence Works

ISBN: 978-1-7384767-0-1

Copyright © 2024 Judy Yorke

Cover illustration and design: Sandra Staufer

For my fellow travellers and adored family Adrian, Kit and Rory.

Chapter 1
The Decision

"Where are you lot off to?"

We've been walking for less than five minutes, trailing our wheelie cases behind us and pretending not to notice that one of them has mysteriously developed a squeaky wheel since we last used it.

We've planned an environmentally-friendly holiday this year and, determined not to fall at the first hurdle, we've decided against taking a taxi to the station.

A friend in her car spots us. She pulls up next to us and winds down her window. We are a motley but distinctive crew, optimistically wearing shorts despite the grey English skies, each with a daypack and wheelie in an uncoordinated range of colours and sizes.

So where *are* we off to exactly? It's not an easy question to answer and we don't quite know what to say. We aren't going to one place, or even one country. We hesitate and glance at each other.

"Europe!" I reply eventually, which is a bit vague and rather grand but is the best short answer I can come up with. "We're going interrailing!"

Interrailing if you've never heard of it (in which case you really do need to hear about it, so I'm extremely glad you're reading this book) is your gateway to Europe. First available in 1972, it's a single ticket that throws open the doors to up to 33 countries. Using the railways of the continent, you can travel pretty much anywhere you choose – up to Oslo or down to Rome, east to Warsaw or west to Lisbon. To great cities, to beautiful mountains, to scenic lakes, to lazy beaches. To zip through countries on speedy inter-cities or take it slowly on scenic, meandering, regional trains.

We've always planned a big trip this year. Our two sons – Kit, 18 and Rory, 16 – have taken A levels and GCSEs respectively, which means we can get away early, avoiding at least part of the school holiday melee.

Our initial plan had been to go to Canada and we'd got as far as buying a guidebook and opening a 'Canada Fund' savings account. But, even without taking the air fare into account, it soon became obvious that it was going to bust our budget. I randomly keyed a few places and dates into booking.com and Airbnb and blanched at the prices. Don't tell the kids, but we've secretly decided that Canada might be an option in a few years' time, when they have flown the nest and we only have to pay for two of us rather than four.

We briefly flirted with the idea of Costa Rica but that seemed all about white water rafting and hanging bridges (my idea of hell) and wildlife spotting (Rory's idea of hell).

So we began to wonder whether we should go somewhere closer to home, with fewer scary creatures and a shorter, cheaper flight. And that set us thinking – how about avoiding airports altogether? Flying just isn't much fun any more and that's even before you get into the whole environmental debate. So how about doing the whole thing by train?

My husband Adrian and I had both been interrailing as students before we'd met and back then you could only go if you were under 26. Even a year ago, it hadn't even crossed my mind that it was an option for middle-aged oldies like us.

Then a Facebook friend posted pictures of her train trip round Italy. "I didn't know you could interrail at our age," I said. Turns out that they'd bought individual tickets rather than interrail passes, but the seed had been sown. Could we do something similar? I searched up the interrail website and discovered to my delight that all age restrictions have been swept away. You can go interrailing at any age and in fact, senior citizens even get a discount. That's something to look forward to in our dotage.

We mentioned it to the boys who were much more enthusiastic about the prospect of a European holiday than I'd expected them to be, especially given the considerably more exotic and far-flung places we'd been talking about.

It was the week before Christmas and on a family day trip to London, we nipped into Stanfords travel bookshop, where we spent an hour, excitement building, looking through various books on European travel. Kit bought the Lonely Planet's Train Travel In Europe guide and we took turns to leaf through it on the train home, reading sections aloud to each other. So many options, so many possibilities. We were mentally planning our trip before we arrived back at Brighton station, which is where our journey would begin seven months later.

When you have the whole of Europe to visit, how do you even start to choose where to go? We decided that each of us should devise an itinerary and present it to the others. Many evenings were spent poring over the map at the front of the book and researching how long it would take to get from A to B.

We set the ground rules: firstly, and most importantly, no planes. We had to do the whole thing there and back by rail. It would just be much more satisfying to do it all by train – more of a challenge, more of an adventure, as well as being much greener. On a practical level, we wouldn't have to worry about luggage weight and liquids and check in times and all the hassle that comes with flying.

Two: the trip must involve at least one night in a sleeper train. I'd slept in little train carriages called couchettes when interrailing before and loved falling asleep in one country and waking in another. An epic rail trip across Europe without a night on a train would seem incomplete somehow.

Three: we wanted to avoid places where we were likely to go on holiday in the future, so no Spain, Greece, Portugal or Italy. This had the advantage of swerving towns and cities that tend to be scorching hot in the summer (very sensibly it turned out as Europe sweated its way through a record heatwave while we were away). It was a holiday to discover places we wouldn't usually go to, or in my case rediscover a couple of cities I'd last visited more than three decades ago.

Four: this must be fitted into three weeks. Adrian and I are both freelance journalists and although we could please ourselves with how long to take off, three weeks seemed about the longest break we could take from work without everyone forgetting who we were. It was also the maximum we thought we could go without earning anything (no holiday pay for us freelancers!) A three-week trip meant we could opt for the 22 day interrail pass and use every last day of it.

Five: we had to do at least one parkrun. Parkruns

are hugely popular 5k runs that take place in open spaces like beaches and, well, parks, in a number of countries across the world on Saturday mornings. We've already done nearly 700 between us and whenever we've been on holiday in the UK, we've tried to fit one in. This did add an extra layer of difficulty to the trip planning, though, as it meant we needed to be within striking distance of at least one and ideally two parkruns in the right city on the right day. Still, who needs simple?

With the rules established, it was time to attempt to come up with an itinerary to present to the others. I drew one up, then changed it, adapted it, and altered it again. It was so hard to decide where NOT to go. I was determined to seize the chance to finally make it to Budapest, which has long been on my bucket list. I really wanted to go to Croatia too. My first list featured Ljubljana, Zagreb and Zurich. Later versions included Lake Bled and Cologne. We didn't make it to any of those in the end. (I don't think a swift change in Zurich really counts).

In their rooms, in front of the TV, at the kitchen table, the others were doing the same. Train Travel In Europe was thumbed and places exclaimed over. Google was consulted on an hourly basis. Dinner talk was of the Black Forest, Frankfurt and Paris. Adrian liked the idea of Bulgaria. Rory wondered if we might go to Athens. We reminded him of Rule Three.

Parkrun was making things even more difficult. It was no good being in Budapest on one of our Saturdays as there was still no parkrun there, despite months of rumours of one starting.

I asked myself whether we should spend three days on a beach to catch our breath a couple of weeks into the trip but reluctantly crossed out potential resorts. With the treasures of Europe to discover, lying on a nondescript beach somewhere seemed a criminal waste of days.

The day before the boys went back to school and college, we convened a family meeting and presented our suggestions. Adrian and I read from scraps of paper, with crossings out and scribbled notes. The boys, from a generation that does everything on screen, both designed PowerPoint presentations complete with maps and statistics, projected on to the TV.

We all had a few places in common – Brussels and perhaps more surprisingly Baden-Baden, which had seized everyone's imagination after getting a mention in The Book.

Somehow, we cobbled everyone's suggestions together and began to fashion a schedule. We had all agreed we'd like to spend a night in Switzerland and the boys were particularly keen on going to Lausanne to visit the Olympic Museum. It's on Lake Geneva so we could swim there too, which ticked the "wild swimming" box.

We manage to fit in Budapest but Croatia had to go – there just wasn't enough time. Rory wanted to start in Brussels so we could spend our first day at the Mini-Europe attraction, which had models of many major European sights and monuments. He thought it would be fun to see everything in miniature on day one before we saw it for real later in the trip.

We didn't need to make a final decision about our itinerary just yet but we did need to buy our interrail tickets as there was a sale on in January offering 10% off. If you think interrailing is a cheap alternative to flying, you're going to be disappointed. The boys were entitled to youth tickets but as fully-fledged adults, Adrian and I had to pay full whack. For the four of us, the tickets came to £1370 – just what we needed on the credit card bill after Christmas. I gave silent thanks to the Canada savings fund as I emptied it.

Buying a ticket sounds straightforward but there were still decisions to be made. These days, you can opt for either a paper interrail ticket or a mobile pass. We chose the latter which you don't have to activate until the first day you travel. This means that you don't have a fixed start date and can change your mind right up to the day you slam your front door shut.

This was just as well as our departure date kept shifting. Rory lucked out in the Wimbledon ticket ballot which pushed everything back a few days. Accommodation in Budapest then soared in price on our new dates. What on earth was going on? Google revealed that we were due to hit town at the same time as the Hungarian Grand Prix. We rescheduled again. We were now doing the original route backwards.

Once we had something approaching a final itinerary, I joined a couple of Facebook groups including the fabulous Interrailing for the Older Crowd, for inspiration, hints, and ideas of what to do in each place.

The most important thing, I gathered, was to book Eurostar tickets as early as possible. Interrailers get a special passholder fare but tickets for these are limited. This meant yet another change of dates and schedule as there were none left for the home leg of our much-rearranged journey. The latest rejig meant we would now get the Eurostar to Brussels and come home from the Netherlands, rather than do them one after the other which was the original plan. I think this was about plan M.

There were still many months before we set off. I dreamed of the summer, of the heat, of sitting in a beer garden nursing a beer as the sun went down. It was a long and damp winter. The cold days and dark evenings lingered, and when summer finally emerged, the boys' exams seemed to go on for ever.

I discovered Vinted and sold a few items to boost the holiday fund. I wrote an article about interrailing when you are older and interviewed a couple of women my age who had done it. They both radiated enthusiasm and told me they couldn't wait to go again.

As summer approached, I had the usual "where are you going for your holiday?" conversations with friends. I was touched by people's enthusiasm for our trip. Just about everyone said it sounded fabulous. A great idea! So many asked where exactly we were going that I could soon recite our route.

Others expressed surprise that our boys still wanted to come on holiday with us. ("You keep paying, I'll keep coming," seems to be our older son's mantra.) He's 18 and will be off to university soon; I was looking forward to some extended and memorable time together.

Many friends reminisced about their own interrailing days. It seems everyone I know did it – I must have bumped into some of them unknowingly at youth hostels in Italy 35 years ago.

I asked myself if I was envious of friends who would be spending a restful fortnight this summer dipping in and out of infinity pools in posh hotels. I admitted to me that yes, I was a bit. We were going on an adventure but one thing it wouldn't be was relaxing. Would we need a holiday when we came back?

"Are you sure you want to spend your entire holiday on a train?" asked my mother who had just come back from a cruise and therefore spent her entire holiday on a boat.

I tinkered with our itinerary. We were supposed to

stay in Brussels for four nights and take day trips to Bruges and Ypres but they both involved going via Ghent. Why not just stay in Ghent for three nights and then in Brussels the last one? I altered the booking. It meant we couldn't go to Mini-Europe on our first day but Rory, knee-deep in Chemistry revision, manfully accepted the change.

I booked reserved seats on a few of the longer journeys as I didn't fancy standing for seven hours. This meant more decisions had to be made – did we want to leave Salzburg for Budapest in the morning or after lunch? Would everyone prefer a direct train or did they mind changing in Vienna?

I renewed our passports, debated whether we needed packing cubes, bought a new hat.

Mostly, I waited impatiently for July.

Chapter 2
The Trip

Day 1: Departure

We are standing on the concourse at Brighton station and I'm gazing around and wondering where everyone bearing luggage is going. Are they nipping up to London overnight, or are they going to Gatwick to jet off on holiday? Is anyone else interrailing and if so, where are they heading to? Does anyone have a longer journey than us? I try and fail to spot any other interrailers.

Our train to London, where we are going to catch the Eurostar, is cancelled. This is not a good start, but there's another train leaving soon afterwards. We've downloaded our mobile tickets, but Adrian can't get his to activate. Another not good start. Once he's managed to sort that out (or more accurately, once the boys have sorted it out for him), we can't get the tickets to open the barriers and have to show our phones to the staff. That's three bad starts and it's only 10am.

The train, probably because of the cancellation, is hot, heaving and horrible. A woman is standing holding her baby so I feel obliged to give up my seat and stand for an uncomfortable 20 minutes. When we finally arrive, sweating, in London, there's a bit of a kerfuffle because our luggage is wedged behind someone else's. When we finally disembark, I'm thoroughly glad to be off the train. Then I realise that's not a good attitude for someone about to travel several thousand kilometres by the same mode of transport over the next three weeks. I give myself a stern talking to.

The last time I got the Eurostar was so long ago it departed from Waterloo, but in 2007 it moved to St Pancras. The station is crowded but the snaking line to check in is well-organised. There are signs showing which queue to join for our train, the 13:01 to Brussels Midi.

I'm surprised to go through passport control on the way out twice – once to leave Britain and once to enter Europe – but that's because there's no passport control at the other end. It's one of the joys of travelling by train. No passport control, no baggage reclaim, no taxi from the airport. Instead, you arrive slap bang in the middle of town ready to start your holiday, and drink your first beer, immediately.

The journey itself is smooth, quick and uneventful and within a couple of hours we're in Brussels. It's so easy, it's almost an anti-climax. I'm used to arriving on holiday with the pilot announcing the weather, and the cabin crew smiling brightly at us as we disembark. Instead, we step off the train to little fanfare.

Brussels station is teeming with people walking briskly and purposefully. We are not among them. We're not staying here as we're off immediately to Ghent, but access to the platform our train is departing from is blocked off. We find an official looking person to ask but too late realise he's a security guard. Eventually we walk a very circuitous route with our squeaky suitcase to find the platform.

Our first introduction to Belgian trains – in fact to European trains – is not a good one.

Whoever designed the steep steps from platform to carriage obviously didn't have a suitcase with them. It's an effort to haul our luggage up and into the compartment.

There are no seats to be had and the train is packed and boiling. People are fanning themselves with hands and books. The doors are taking ages to close. Gangs of young men are walking through the carriage and then getting off and it's making me feel nervous. I'm a bit paranoid because I've read that Brussels Midi is rife with pickpockets. On one of the Facebook pages, someone reported that they didn't even make it out of the station before their bag was stolen. We eventually set off, all possessions intact, but we are standing in the gap between two carriages and we're in everybody's way.

After a change at Gent-Sint-Pieters, it's only a few minutes to our stop, Gent-Dampoort, and when we emerge there are two things we notice. First, the enormous bike-park – there are dozens and dozens of bicycles parked outside. It's a truly impressive sight though I have to admit that my first thought is to wonder how anyone ever finds their own after a long day at work.

Secondly, it seems the area around the station is being rebuilt too. There are cranes and barriers everywhere. Our hotel is supposed to be about five minutes' walk from the station – but we follow diversion signs all around the houses for about 15 minutes, our case squeaking the whole way.

Eventually, we arrive. The Aparthotel Adagio Access Gent Centrum Dampoort to give it its full and rather wordy name is a budget hotel but it's fabulous – it's brand new, it's spacious and it's sparkling. We're pleased to see a bar and an airy lounge area. I hadn't really noticed those on the website. Outside there's a good-sized and very pleasant terrace which backs on to a river. The receptionists are friendly and welcome us to "the Venice of the North" (which turns out to be a slight exaggeration.) Our studio room is lovely. It has a big fridge and a little hob, a decent size bathroom and very comfortable beds.

We'd planned to cook in tonight, the logic being that we'll have to do this some nights to save cash, and we might as well get the first one out of the way immediately. We've even lugged (well, Adrian's lugged) pasta and a heavy jar of tomato sauce all the way from home to avoid having to hunt down a supermarket. But by the time we'd got to Ghent station number one, we'd decided we couldn't be bothered. We want to stretch our legs, explore the town and start our holiday, especially as the weather is so warm.

It's a 15-minute stroll into town, and it gets prettier and more atmospheric as we approach the centre. We have our first Belgian beer of the holiday with dinner (a build-your-own pita) and then wander to the beautiful quayside with medieval buildings. Ghent is gorgeous – all canals and bridges and olde worlde architecture. You can even sit on the quayside, dangling your legs over the water. We join the hordes doing exactly that.

We haven't booked breakfast at the hotel because as we have a mini kitchen, there's no reason not to make our own. This seemed a good idea until we realise we have arrived late on a Saturday and most shops are closed. After-dinner entertainment involves trying and failing to find a supermarket. The first one that is open only has cereal of the chocolate variety. We triumphantly find another one which is open 24/7 but when we go in it seems you need to download an app before you can buy anything. And to download the app, you need ID. How very 21st century and how very inconvenient. We eventually find one that opens tomorrow morning.

Back at the hotel, we treat ourselves to another beer and decide what time we're getting the train tomorrow. The boys play a viciously competitive game of table tennis.

Steps: 20,683; distance walked: 13.6km (mostly round the backstreets of Ghent); trains: four; beers: two. Minutes of mild panic getting Adrian's interrail ticket to work: several.

Day 2: Bruges

One of the reasons for staying in Ghent is that it's very easy to get to other places we want to visit. It's kind of the Birmingham New Street of Belgium. Today (a bit later than planned as we have to wait for the supermarket that doesn't just sell chocolate cereal to open) we are off to Bruges which is a half hour train ride away.

It's our first double decker train which, although we have a combined age of 143, excites us immensely so of course we happily climb the steps and sit at the top level. This train is so much better than yesterday's – it's not crowded and we don't have luggage to drag up the precipitous stairs. We fairly dance up the steps and I grab the window seat.

Bruges is a very cute place and, like an annoying toddler, it definitely knows it. It's everything you'd expect it to be, with cobbled streets, horses and carriages, old fashioned houses, canals, boat trips and chocolate shops. We even spot a windmill.

First things first – coffee and pastries – in Markt, the main square. It's a great place for people-watching, which is one of the great joys of travel. There are plenty of British people here but I hear German and French voices too. Restored by cakes and cappuccino, we saunter through the city, posing for photos in all combinations (me and Kit; Kit and Adrian; Adrian, Rory and me) beside various canals. It's starting to rain so I suggest Rory might like to think about getting his waterproof out of his bag. He stops to do so and nearly gets knocked over by a passing horse which is pulling a carriage laden with tourists. That would have been an interesting one to explain to the insurance company.

Lunch – well it has to be Belgian fries, doesn't it? We make the mistake of adding extra salt without realising that the chips have already been well-seasoned. The guy behind the counter decides to tell us this just as we're finishing adding extra salt to the final chip cone. I think he also wants us to buy water.

It's still drizzling lethargically as we stroll through

the Begijnhof, a calm garden flanked by white houses. The Bruges website tells us it was founded in 1245. Today, Benedictine nuns, as well as some single women, live there. It's a very peaceful place and we have no wish to shatter it. We talk in whispers and avoid walking on the grass. Afterwards we sit by the river for a while, the strains of a rock concert wafting over to us.

We spend the rest of the afternoon wandering in and out of the chocolate shops. There are so many and the sweet smell of cocoa hangs in the damp air. And it's not just chocolate. I can't take my eyes off the huge, fat rolls of marzipan in a myriad of flavours – there's strawberry, rum & raisin, citrus and many more. We splurge on glossy dark chocolate slabs, unadulterated chocolate marzipan and soft, adorable truffles.

We also search out our first fridge magnet of the holiday. It takes a good 10 minutes, several arguments and about five shops to choose one that is just right – beer, a row of shops, a canal and a horse-drawn carriage to remind us of Rory's near-miss. Fridge magnet hunting is to become a theme of the trip. Rory also collects snow globes but he has to be selective as he isn't going to have case space for one from each location.

In the late afternoon, fridge magnet safely in pocket, we make the easy journey back to Ghent. By now we have sussed the four-minute-direct-to-the-hotel route from the station avoiding the building work. We cook our boring-but-very-cheap dinner in our studio but the evening is young and we head into town afterwards for beer, ice-cream and in Kit's case both. I can't believe how clean the streets are here compared to back home. There's no litter, no bags of rubbish.

When we get back to the hotel it's nearly 10pm and still both light and warm, so we sit outside with another beer.

I had always thought of this as a trip rather than a holiday, especially in Belgium with its UK-like climate. But here we are sipping our drinks and enjoying our complimentary nibbles on a lovely summer's evening as the fairy lights twinkle and conversation buzzes animatedly around us. We could be in Majorca. Almost.

Steps: 32,550; distance walked:21.4km.

Surprise(s) of the day: double decker trains; seven handmade Belgian chocolates for €3.

Day 3: Ypres

We're all fascinated by history so we've decided to take a trip to Ypres (French) / Ieper (Dutch) to see the First World War battlefields and cemeteries. You need to book a tour of Ypres if you don't have your own car as it's too far to walk to all the sites. In any case, it's always good to have a guide for this sort of trip as you find out so much more. We've paid €45 each for a four-hour Grand Tour.

Getting the train there is trickier than it needs to be. The information boards on Belgian platforms tend to give the destination but not necessarily all the stops in between. Thank goodness for the incredibly useful SNCB (Belgian railways) app. Once we've worked out the platform, we realise that the train splits en route, with only part of it going on to Ypres. I ask the conductor if we are in the right section. "I don't know – we haven't decided yet," he says helpfully.

Despite everything, we successfully arrive in Ypres where we set about the seemingly simple task of getting a sandwich before our afternoon tour. All the restaurants appear to be serving full-on lunches rather than a quick sarnie so we look for a bakery. It's Monday and most things are shut. We eventually find a bakery and establish through a bit of gesticulating and a lot of bad French that they only sell bread and cakes rather than, for instance, a roll with fromage et jambon. So we buy crusty rolls and delicious little tarts and decide not to worry about the lack of protein or vitamin C.

Given our love of people-watching, we're looking forward to joining a big tour group. But when the minibus rolls up, we're told there's only us. We feel momentarily disappointed but then pretty chuffed to be having an exclusive tour at non-exclusive prices.

Our guide is incredibly knowledgeable and we spend a sombre but fascinating few hours touring war cemeteries, memorials, battlegrounds and trenches. She tells us about the poison gas attacks and the young boys who lied about their age to join up.

I know a bit about the triage system during the First World War thanks to testing Rory for his GCSE history but am shocked at how incredibly small and dark the holding stations are. You can only stand in there and imagine it teeming with injured soldiers and doctors trying desperately to save their lives or patch them up ready to return to the frontline.

The rows of graves – some higgledy-piggledy, some uniform – are well-cared for and our guide seems on first name terms with some of the gardeners. The cemeteries are immaculate. At least these fallen troops are being well-treated in death. But there are heartbreaking numbers of graves of unknown soldiers, with the simple moniker "Known unto God."

We press on to the Langemark Cemetery, where German soldiers are buried. It's a painfully large site. Hitler paid a triumphant visit here in 1940 when the Germans occupied the area. Many other German war graves were moved here during the 1950s, to reduce the number of cemeteries which needed to be maintained. There's now a mass grave of unidentified German soldiers.

It's all very sobering so we enjoy the moments of light relief, especially the clear rivalry between the tour guides with a lot of tutting if one secures a favoured spot at a location to give their talk. Our guide fiercely tells some schoolkids not to walk on the grass where there are so many buried soldiers underneath. They obey immediately. It's that sort of place, or she's got that sort of tone. Probably both.

We also visit some of the memorials and I am particularly taken with the Saint Julien memorial, which commemorates Canadian soldiers. The imposing and striking "Brooding Soldier" design was selected after a competition. It's the bowed head and shoulders of a soldier on top of a tall, slender 11m column.

Our afternoon has been very quiet, with little but the voice of our guide and the rustling of the wind in the trees on the massive battlefields. Afterwards, it's good to be back in the hubbub of modern Belgium. The restaurant recommended by our guide is closed so we take our chances on another one, De Kollebloeme. We sit outside in the spacious, elegant but calm main square and the food is just fabulous. I order Flemish stew which is beef steeped in beer and it is fantastic. Rory manages the world's most chocolatey pudding without any help (we did offer). The staff are charming and helpful. When we leave, they shower us with sweets. Our pockets are bulging with them and they'll be eaten gratefully on long train journeys later on. The restaurant bill is €115, less than £25 a head: three weeks later it is to win our "favourite meal of the holiday" award.

We're hanging around Ypres because we want to go

to the Menin Gate Last Post ceremony, which takes place every night at 8pm. The Gate bears the names of more than 54,000 soldiers who died here during the First World War but who have no known grave.

The Gate itself is being renovated and it's under scaffolding but it doesn't affect the atmosphere. The ceremony takes place in front of the Gate. It's thronged and as I'm only 4ft 10in, I can't see over everyone's heads to view what's happening. So I close my eyes and take in all the sounds instead.

I'm just expecting to hear a bugle, but there's also a simple reading of the poem 'They shall grow not old'. It's spine-tingling. There are loads of kids here on school trips – back home schools haven't yet broken up – and some of them are laying wreaths. We inspect them afterwards. "Lest we forget. King's Academy Easthampstead Park, Bracknell," says one. I think every school kid should come here. We are to learn later, in Munich, that German children are taken by their schools to see a concentration camp. Lest we forget: there is surely no more important lesson.

There's only one train an hour back to Ghent at 15 past the hour and there's no way we are going to make it. It seems almost deliberately timed to ensure you don't sprint away from the ceremony. Instead, we walk away slowly, quietly and thoughtfully.

Steps: 14,614 (9.6km); marks out of 10 for Flemish stew: 9.5. (Very short) conversations in French:1

Day 4: Brussels

This morning, we leave genteel Ghent for busy Brussels. We've only got one day and night in the capital, so we make an early start with the 8.25am train. Dutch and French are spoken in different parts of Belgium and as we get closer to Brussels, I realise that the train notifications change from impenetrable (to me!) Dutch to "I can get the gist of this" French.

It's a bit of an effort to find our hotel, the Meininger Gare du Midi, which as its name suggests is right by the station. Which exit is it? I wish hotels would put this on their "how to get here" information.

We make it by 9.30. I check in to the hotel in French (I've practised "I learnt French many years ago and I've forgotten most of it") and we manage to have a conversation. The receptionist asks for my passport and I find it, managing a joke about it probably being the last of the four I get out of my bag (it is). We establish that even though it's so early, we can access our room now for an extra €15.

I make her repeat this several times in case I have mistaken "15" for "50". I was expecting to have to pay to leave our luggage here so this seems a real bargain. She compliments me on my French, which she says is very good, but I suspect she means "very good in comparison to most English people who can't say anything other than merci." I feel very proud of myself. I love Brussels already.

The boys have decided our itinerary today – they want to go first to Mini-Europe, which contains to-scale iconic monuments and buildings of all the European member states. Oh, plus the UK, which must have given them a major headache and been the cause of endless meetings when we voted to leave. Who could have blamed them for wanting to remove us lock stock and barrel?

Mini-Europe is right at the end of the metro line by Heysel Stadium and a bit out of town.

It's fascinating to see which monuments they have chosen for each country. For Belgium, we're pleased to spot, among others, a mini Ypres complete with graveyard and a perfect tiny Canadian Memorial. There's also Brussels of course, and the medieval buildings of Ghent where we spent our first evening.

In Italy, Adrian seizes the opportunity to be pictured trying to push over the Leaning Tower of Pisa with his little finger while I get up close to the Arc de Triomphe in France. And – well played Brussels! – they really take the mick out of the UK with a little customs checkpoint area marked with a dotted red line as you approach it. There's the Houses of Parliament complete with Brexit protests, but we're a bit surprised to see Bath's Royal Crescent rather than Oxford or Buckingham Palace, plus a Cotswold village called Bibury, which I've never even heard of.

The boys love it here so much I'm worried that all we'll see of Brussels is models of it rather than the real thing, but we drag them out of the heat with the promise of a panini in the café. Our next port of call, the Atomium, is next door. Designed for Expo 1958, it's a futuristic steel building made up of a very strange collection of large metal balls connected by tubes. I bought tickets last night so we can skip that queue, but we join a long and rather slow-moving line to go up the lift to the top viewing gallery. Mini-Europe looks incredibly mini from up here incidentally – how did we spend so long there?

Once we've come back down again, we visit the different balls with escalators and travelators whisking you between them. There's plenty about the history of the building, with some of the globes offering mesmerising light and sound effects. It's fun, but it does remind me slightly of the O2 when it was first built – an amazing building which no one was quite sure what to do with.

The metro system is very easy to get the hang of and we head back confidently to the centre. We are in dire need of waffles – no we're not bored of them yet – and coffee before we return to the tourist trail. In the café I ask for a bottle of water but my French deserts me and I thoroughly confuse both the staff and myself by asking for "agua mineral sin gas." Damn those Spanish evening classes!

Grand-Place is, all the guide books tell us, a must-see in Brussels. A UNESCO World Heritage site, it's a huge square edged by stunning, imposing buildings including the city hall. Well today it turns out it's a can't-really-see. There's a concert taking place, with the massive stage obscuring one side of the square and there are so many people standing watching it's difficult to walk past them. (Great concert though). Nearby Manneken Pis, the "weeing boy" statue, has a predictable crowd surrounding it. But just like the Mona Lisa in Paris, it's so much smaller than you'd expect. We are decidedly underwhelmed.

By now we are flagging. We've had an early start, we've walked miles and it's surprisingly hot. I'd like to go to the European Parliament but I am in a minority of one and time is ticking on so we're probably too late to do a tour anyway. We have a beer – a dark, nutty, wonderful beer – while we consider our options. It is astonishing how much this single glass of beer revives us. With a new spring in our step, we decide we'd like to go to the Royal Quarter so we set off on foot. It turns out to be an excellent decision and, out of the main tourist trap, we see Brussels in a new light. It's a lovely area, green, serene and graceful, with tuneful busking, elegant statues and a fabulous view of the city.

We're not sure where to go for dinner as all the

restaurants look either chainy or touristy. It's our last night in Belgium and we want something more memorable.

Rory gets out his phone, presses a few keys and says to follow him, which we dutifully do. As we enter a park he says, "100 metres to go!" I'm getting more and more confused about where this mysterious restaurant could be and am beginning to doubt Google Maps. But suddenly there it is in front of us. Woodpecker is an outdoor restaurant, a kind of beer garden really, right there in the park, with long tables under the trees and fairy lights strung between them. On a warm summer's evening like today, it's idyllic. (Less idyllic are the camping-style toilets, which, to add insult to injury, you have to pay for).

Plenty of other people have obviously had the same idea as the queue for food is long and the blackboard menu has an ominous number of crossings out. All that's left is hotdogs and chips. Hotdogs and chips will do just fine. And beer, of course.

Afterwards, we walk back to our hotel, passing Brussels Midi station which is not known to be the most salubrious area. Brussels is so much dirtier than Ghent. We get a bit lost and I'm slightly uncomfortable and relieved to get to the hotel. The Meininger – a chain which I'd never heard of before this trip – is a cross between a budget hotel and a youth hostel with a mix of private rooms and dorms. We have a private en suite with a double bed and a bunk bed and it's modern, clean and spacious. There's a bar and a guest kitchen and it's a good and convenient place to spend a night.

We settle into the bar for a coffee and spot a young people's choir that was also at our hotel in Ghent last night. The bar is noisy and there's some drama as an ambulance turns up. The medics start talking to a woman at the next table and we feel uncomfortable as we can overhear the conversation.

It seems a cue to retire to our room for an early night, as we are up with the larks tomorrow.

So farewell Belgium. We've loved your food, your hospitality and your unexpectedly tropical weather. You lose a point for your trains, which you need crampons to clamber on to.

Steps: 31,602 (20.8km); calories used up: 2,220 (all "spent" on beer, chips and hotdog); fridge magnets purchased to date: four.

Question of the day: How do cobbled streets and bikes co-exist so happily in Belgium?

Day 5: Brussels to Munich

Well, it was a good plan in theory. Up (very) early for the 6:23am Brussels to Frankfurt train, a quick change there at 10ish and in Munich by 1.30pm.

We'd tiptoed out of the hotel before 6am, hoping

the squeaky wheel wouldn't wake everyone up, and stocked up on rolls and croissants for breakfast at the station supermarket.

Now, after negotiating the surprisingly crowded platform and locating our reserved seats, we've found space for our luggage, opened our kindles / put in our ear-pods and gasped at the number of scouts on the train. We are just settling in for the three-and-a-half-hour journey when a guard arrives and makes an announcement.

Everyone around us starts to gather their belongings, which definitely isn't a good sign. Then he repeats it in English. The bad news: the air conditioning unit in our carriage is broken and it is apparently dangerous to stay here. The good news: we can move to first class where there is plenty of space. The bad news: it's at the other end of the train.

We relocate relatively cheerfully to first class with its wide, deep seats and extra leg room. It's an unexpected treat even though we can't all sit together (or maybe because we can't all sit together). I find myself in a single seat next to the window. Hurrah! I'm not used to first class so look around for the personal butler, and failing that, the free coffee. Neither materialises, so I bury myself in my book.

It appears that the scouts haven't managed to all find seats so they are sitting outside the toilet when I want to go there. They make space for me to open the door without complaint — they must have been doing this every couple of minutes throughout the whole journey – and smile. They are certainly a great advert for the scout movement. I bet they fall over themselves to help old ladies cross the road.

According to various Facebook groups I've been following with increasing interest over the last few months, trains from Brussels to Germany are notorious for being cancelled or delayed. (And, I later discover, for having malfunctioning air conditioning units.)

I'm really hoping that our 5.45am alarm doesn't turn out to be a colossal waste of time (and sleep). To ratchet up the tension, we've only got 15 minutes for our connection at Frankfurt Airport. There is a handy but anxiety-inducing information screen on the train showing where we are, what the next station is and how late we are. We're about 10 minutes behind schedule.

The DB (Deutsche-Bahn, the German train operator) app shows that our next train is running late too. I'm really hoping we'll get it. While an interrail ticket means a missed connection isn't a disaster as you can just jump on the next train, it does mean we'd lose our reserved seats and, more importantly, valuable time in Munich. We've only got a night there so every minute counts.

The app shows our connecting train getting later... and later...and later – and then it's cancelled. There's an hour or so until the next one so we stretch our legs, buy sandwiches and pastries for lunch and go to the ticket office to attempt to change our reservation (too late apparently).

We manage to get seats on the next train easily enough but when I glance at the information screen, I do a double take. We're going to take an extra two and a half hours to get to Munich.

It turns out that there was a massive storm in Germany yesterday, damaging the track, which means we have to do a huge diversion. The train staff announce free ice creams for the kids (at 16 is Rory a kid? No matter as he won't go up and get one anyway as it's "so embarrassing".) There's also free water and biscuits for everyone (I am not embarrassed to go and get them) and a good spirit of togetherness on the train. There is much debate about changing trains but somehow a group decision is made to stay on this one.

Something was bound to go wrong on this trip and I'm hoping this is it. We eventually limp in to Munich at 17:40, a mere four-and-a-bit hours later than we'd expected.

As we have so little time in Munich (and even less time now), I've booked us accommodation just about as close as I can to the station. Oh, and somewhere as cheap as possible too as all we are going to do there is sleep. Step forward the 4U youth hostel!

I've been to Munich before, 30+ years ago, on my

first interrail trip. Back then we stayed at the world's most inhospitable youth hostel: bars on the windows, a loud-speaker waking you up at 7am and a man conducting random checks on the breakfast queue to inspect your breakfast token. It was miserable at the time but has been something to look back on with hilarity ever since.

I have to admit that part of the reason I chose this rather than other budget options is a nod to that. It's funny to think that several decades later, I'm back at a Munich youth hostel, husband and teenagers in tow, even if it isn't the same one.

When we arrive at 4U, I'm slightly alarmed to be issued with breakfast tokens just like we were all those years ago. However we're also given vouchers for a free drink at the bar so, with the promise of our first hotel breakfast AND a nice glass of beer this evening, I'm pretending to myself it's the youth hostel equivalent of an all-inclusive wristband.

After our tortuous journey and stupidly early start, we're all feeling slightly worn out. Munich is a big, historic city and as we don't have much time to explore, we're not quite sure where to start. A friend who's a German teacher and Munich afficionado has suggested a particular beer garden for dinner. The Hofbraeukeller is a half hour walk through the city centre which seems an ideal way of getting some exercise and seeing something of the city.

The route takes us through Marienplatz, Munich's central square and as it's just before 7pm, we hang about a bit and gaze hopefully at the glockenspiel in the town hall. It's a strange building – so black in places it almost looks like there's been a fire there in the past. But disappointingly it doesn't perform on the hour so we press on. We go into the Bayern Munich club shop, glance at the prices, and quickly leave.

The Hofbraeukeller garden is massive, with loads of tables and a merry atmosphere. Everyone is enjoying the warm summer evening. It takes a few minutes to work it all out. Instead of table menus, there are various food counters where you can select your dinner, puddings, and of course beer. It's all self-service – a sort of canteen if you like – and there's no standing on ceremony. You grab a tray, choose your food outlet, ask for what you want and cart it back to your table (rather precariously given the size of the beer glasses). The place is full of locals, which is always a good sign.

I have the schnitzel which is nice but unspectacular. Kit lets me try some of his pork steak and it is sensational. I don't know what it's been marinated in but it's fantastic. All in all, it's a memorable evening. We're in a much happier mood by the time we make it back to the 4U.

As we get back, the latest storm starts. The first raindrops fall as we push open the door to the hostel.

We think about spending our free tokens in the bar

but we're tired, the bar is noisy and – would you believe it – the youth hostel is full of young people. I feel ancient. Instead, we head off to the fifth floor and bed.

The storm is brewing itself into a frenzy and there's a lightning display outside. Fingers crossed there's no more train drama tomorrow!

Minutes on train: 632; steps: a surprisingly respectable 17,458 (11.5km) given the above. Blisters:1 (fourth toe, right foot).

Day 6: Munich to Salzburg

We'd hoped for a good night's sleep after yesterday's early start but if there are any blinds on our windows, they've been cunningly disguised, so light pours in in the small hours. The boys get up early for a run. They discover that Munich (or "our" part of it at least) is a lousy city to run in because there are so many cyclists to dodge. There are also many roads and you're not supposed to cross them unless the pedestrian traffic light is green, so it's all very stop-start and slightly unsatisfying. They run to Olympic Park a couple of miles away, take photos of each other by the Olympic rings and return to base.

There are four tiny sachets of shower gel / shampoo in the bathroom so I am the only one able to wash both hair and body. One aptly small advantage of being under 5ft tall. This morning the lift is broken so it's a bit of effort to drag our cases down five flights of stairs to the luggage room (still, it's easier than hoicking it UP five flights, I think, as I smile weakly at the unlucky guests doing exactly that.)

After a big family debate last night – should we go to Salzburg early doors as planned or spend some time in Munich as we haven't really seen any of it yet? – we've decided on the latter and searched up a free walking tour. We know from experience that these tours are a great way of discovering a city in a few hours. For the uninitiated, there's no official payment for these but at the end you give whatever tip you think the guide deserves.

It never occurred to me that you'd need to book a free tour, as I'd always assumed it was a case of the more the merrier, or the more the richer for the lucky tour guide. However when we arrive, we are told it's full. We're directed to another guide, who has space as the tour is about to start and a few people haven't turned up.

The tour starts at Marienplatz, and is timed so you can actually see the glockenspiel at 11am – turns out, it doesn't emerge every hour. It's something like 12 minutes long and there are motorised figures with jousting and all sorts. It's very high up and there's quite a lot of neck craning involved. I like it but I have to be honest and say it could be a bit shorter.

Our guide, Ricardo, is from Peru. He's lived here in Munich for a few years but hasn't learned German, which is why he gives tours in English. He tells us he hasn't had much sleep the night before as he was up writing his dissertation. If this is a tired Ricardo, I can't imagine how energetic a well-rested Ricardo would be. He's full of wit and engaging stories.

Fascinating fact of the day: when the opera house was on fire, it coincided with a water shortage. Volunteers were given beer to douse it with but ...let's just say the opera house burned down.

Ricardo keeps picking on Rory when he discovers he is 16. "Did you know you can drink beer in Munich at 16?" Yes he does and, despite being a firm teetotaller at home, he tried it last night (we were in a famous beer garden, in Munich; it would have been rude not to.) It is apparently disgusting; I suspect this will not always be the case.

Ricardo also explains to us about the traditional dress for women called a dirndl. You could tell whether a woman was single, married or widowed from the position of her sash, which must have come in very useful in pre-Tinder days.

We leave Ricardo a decent tip and, for lunch, retrace our footsteps to an open-air food market in a nearby square which we had walked past on our tour. Adrian wants a panini but the boys and I have our eyes on the pretzels. The teens go off to find them and come back with three huge specimens. "We didn't realise how big they were till we'd bought them," they say lamely when I point out that they're so massive we could have shared one. There is no way we can finish them but we do our best. They are salty, chewy and delicious.

We're quite pleased with what we've managed to fit in in just a few hours in Munich. We've seen some of the main sights (thanks to Ricardo) including the square where Hitler spoke to the masses, and learned a little about modern Germany. I'm fascinated and appalled by his tales of the students who were executed for their anti-Nazi leaflets. We've also seen the little alley where people would make a detour to avoid having to give a compulsory salute to a Nazi monument. Today they are commemorated with golden cobblestones.

We'd love to spend a little more time here, and we're sad not to have had time to visit the Englischer Garten and watch the surfers, which had been on our original itinerary.

But Salzburg is calling so we retrieve our suitcases from the 4U luggage room and walk the three minutes to the crowded station. We are feeling like true interrailers now, adept at finding platforms, confidently sourcing a spot for our luggage and expertly toggling our tickets. The train is easy and quick – a mere 90 minutes. I don't even bother to open my kindle, though

I do nibble more of the pretzel that I'd stuffed in my bag.

I'm a bit nervous about our Salzburg hotel. Someone on Interrailing for the Older Crowd stayed there last month and posted a picture of it – very close to a sex shop. Just what you want on a family trip. "Don't worry, it's fine," she'd replied when I anxiously enquired. We've selected it, inevitably, for location and price and now I'm worried it's a bit too cheap and I've booked us into the middle of the red-light district.

Turns out the hotel is at least 50m from the sex shop and everyone pretends not to notice it as we walk past. The hotel is slightly old-fashioned looking but clean and attractive and the receptionist couldn't be nicer. Rory uses his GCSE German to say that we have a room booked for four people and the receptionist replies in English, adding with a smile "but he can practise on me if he wants." Our room is a decent size with a big fan, (though no aircon), and a separate toilet and small bathroom.

It is immediately obvious that Salzburg is gorgeous: it's elegant, calm and graceful. There are multiple bridges of different styles across the Salzach river, including a "lovelock" bridge. Lovers have put colourful padlocks all over the bridge with their own names and those of their amours to signify their eternal devotion.

We stroll through the colourful landscaped Mirabell gardens with its bizarre dwarf statues, and wander along the river into town for dinner. We don't know what to eat or where. Kit does some googling and finds a recommended place nearby but the schnitzel there is veal which we won't eat, and there's nothing else Rory fancies.

Google comes to the rescue again and we join the queue outside the Zwettler's restaurant (4.5 out of 5 on Trip Advisor). A queue is always a good sign (or maybe just a sign that everyone else has read the same reviews). After 20 minutes or so, we're in.

Here, and in other places on this trip, instead of saying, "What would you like?" waiters ask, "Have you found something?" which always makes me want to say "no" to see how they would react.

Instead, we reply "yes" with enthusiasm and order our food – massive schnitzels (everything has been enormous today) for the boys and beef stew for us. It's good but Ypres still has the edge. Adrian knocks his coffee over and the staff tell us not to worry as they mop up, replacing it free of charge.

We admire the sun setting over the city's fort as we walk back to the hotel pretending not to notice the sex shop.

Salzburg, I've only known you for a few hours but I think I'm already in love.

Steps: 26,748 (17.6k); number of us it takes to eat a single slice of Sacher torte: four; different nationalities on our Munich tour: nine, including a disproportionate number of Australians.

Question of the day: can you drink the bathroom water here? Of course, say reception, it comes from the mountain. There is no better water.

Day 7: Salzburg

The day gets off to a bad start when Adrian, who has type 1 diabetes, wakes up and realises that the blood glucose monitor he wears on his arm isn't working. Well it *is* working, but the app on his phone has stopped communicating with it. This means that he has no idea what his blood sugar level is and how much insulin to give himself. Just what you want when you're several hundred miles from home.

He tries to reload the app but it says "not available in your country." Great! I have visions of spending the day nipping from country to country (oh the joys of an interrail ticket) trying to find somewhere it IS available. Germany is just across the border but if that doesn't work, it's quite a long way to Italy...

A quick look at Twitter (as it still was then) reveals it isn't just Adrian – the app has stopped working for other diabetics in the UK. Seems an update has caused problems and the UK diabetic community is not happy. The UK diabetic community is also incredibly helpful, practical and resourceful. Someone has worked out what to do and explained on Twitter. After half an hour of mild panic, it's up and running again. Thanks to the marvellous person on Twitter, we don't have to spend the day wandering from country to country to download the app.

Today is a bit different as I'm going in one direction – The Sound of Music Tour to be exact – while the menfolk go off in another, to nearby Hallein. When we were planning the trip, the boys were keen to go on a mountain coaster. Usually just open in the summer season, these allow you to hurtle down a mountain at great speed in a kind of toboggan on a metal track. A teenager's idea of heaven. The one here has the advantage of being near Hallein salt mine, so you can do both on a day trip.

Now I don't mind the prospect of zipping down a mountain, though I suspect I would apply the brake on the toboggan rather more than the boys. However, I am rather less than keen on the thought of going up it. The only option for this seems to be a chair lift and the thought of that is terrifying as I hate heights. I feel dizzy, sick and sweaty at the very idea of it.

However I do love the idea of doing a Sound of Music tour which is very definitely not on anyone else in the family's "to do" list. So after breakfast they wave me off.

It's getting hot so I'm pleased to be sitting on a nice cool bus. Everyone is in high spirits, the view out of the window is spectacular – even if I don't have a window seat– and there are some loud communal renditions of

Do-Re-Mi led by our tour guide Simon. I can't sing for toffee but no-one knows me here so I join in with gusto. It's good that the boys are several miles away as they would be mortified. After a week of fairly intense family time, it is also slightly wonderful to have some space to myself.

The tour features a lot of "this is where Maria walked up the path" and "this is where the boat capsized" moments, with extra stops at some stunning beauty spots. The house where the family lived in the film is now a luxury hotel, which means we can't go and press our noses up against the window.

I'm particularly enjoying the anecdotes, including the fact that if the Trapps really had escaped over the mountain, they'd actually have ended up in Germany – right at Hitler's Eagle's Nest. In real life, they escaped by train just before the border closed.

Our furthest point is a scenic town called Mondsee. It's here (spoiler alert) that Maria and Captain von Trapp's wedding was filmed. The coach draws into a car park and we are walked the 10 minutes to the church, with pleas to remember the way back. Having no sense of direction, I stare very hard at any landmarks.

I wander into the cool church and then back out into the town, enjoying the solitude, and buy an ice cream and fridge magnet. A wedding party is winding its way through the streets, with many guests in traditional Austrian costume. They pose for photos by the shimmering lake, so when they've finished, I saunter over to have a look at it and take some pictures before going back to the coach.

Ten minutes after our planned departure time, the bus is far from full and our tour guide is looking increasingly worried. There are seven people missing. After a call to the office, we set off without them. Simon picks up the microphone and addresses the "elephant in the room," saying we really can't wait any longer. The office will get in touch with them and we'll drop their bags off back in Salzburg. The coach pulls away.

The "survivors" watch a documentary as we wend our way back to Salzburg. Our final stop on the tour is Mirabell Gardens, where Maria and the children danced around the fountain and up and down the steps.

With the tour finished, I buy a Salzburg card. These get you into most of the city's many attractions, as well as a free ride on buses. The longer you stay, the cheaper it works out at per day AND there's 10% off for interrailers. My two-day pass is a bargain €35.

The boys send a few photos and then message to say the toboggan is such fun they're going to go on it again and will be back late. So I go off alone to visit Mozart's birthplace in Getreidegasse in the centre of the city. It's on a shopping street, wedged in between tourist shops and some high street clothes stores. I gather from my tour of the house that Mozart was a well-dressed dude so I'm sure he wouldn't be impressed. There is loads of really interesting information in the house about Mozart and his family. His mum was apparently a bit of a beauty.

I rendezvous with the boys in the early evening. They loved the toboggan but I make them tell me about the mine too. Were they really thinking this trip was all about fun rather than education? Apparently, they had to get dressed up in overalls for warmth – it being underground and everything. There were slides from one part of the mine to another, a boat ride AND a train ride, a quick trip underground back to Germany plus – for a bit of a reality check – a slightly dull explanation of the history of salt extraction. They have been given tiny salt shakers as a memento which they are trying hard not to lose.

We have consumed so much meat recently that tonight we go to an Italian restaurant to eat margherita pizzas. And fail entirely to go vegetarian when the family at the table next to us are munching their way through a huge mixed platter of Parma ham, salami and olives. We have what they are having.

Steps: 30,398 (20km); number of blisters on one toe (mine) three.

Fact of the day: in The Sound of Music, Christopher Plummer couldn't rip up the Nazi flag in dress rehearsals so it had to be perforated to make it easier.

Question of the day: where did the Missing Seven on my tour get to and how did they get back?

Day 8: Salzburg

My legs are aching with all the walking, I have a toe-sized blister and it's promising to be 35 degrees today so there's an obvious thing to do this morning – parkrun!

As parkrun enthusiasts our trip has, to a certain extent, been built around them by making sure we are in situ to fit in two on this trip. If you have never heard of parkrun, it's a 5k timed run that takes place in parks – and other open spaces like beaches – across the world. The joy of parkrun is that there's a place for you whether you sprint round in 15 minutes or stroll round in an hour.

Parkrun, which started around 20 years ago, is most popular in the UK, where it originated, but you can also do a parkrun on a Saturday morning everywhere from Johannesburg to Sydney. Go on holiday to the likes of Canada, or Finland, or Japan, or Singapore or the US, and if you plan carefully, you'll be able to get your weekly parkrun fix.

Salzburg's parkrun is at Hellbrunn and it's a bus ride away. As we wait for the bus outside the train station, we spot other people who look like parkrunners (well, who else would be wearing running kit and getting the same bus as us?) and have a brief chat. The bus picks up others who are definitely off there too as they're wearing distinctive parkrun wristbands. This is A Good Thing as although my tour bus stopped at Hellbrunn yesterday, I am not sure where the parkrun is. It means we can follow them off the bus and then to find the start of the parkrun itself.

Our home parkrun in Brighton usually has well over 400 runners but we know this is much smaller and today there are 35. The parkrun is fairly deep into the park, and we follow the others through an avenue of trees.

The volunteers – those vital cogs who put up the signs and welcome new runners and scan barcodes to give you your finish time – are extremely friendly. They give the run briefing in English. It's a scenic three-lap course in this stunning park, with a glimpse of the mountains at one point. I force myself to slow down because of the heat and because I want to take it all in. Well, that's my excuse and I'm sticking to it. Kit and Rory ignore these niceties and speed round, lapping me. Rory's first to finish (no one "wins" parkrun) and Kit is second. I continue to plod, enjoying the moments of shade under the trees.

It's so small that you get an individual round of applause when you cross the finish line. I come 19th – my first ever top 20 finish! Also, my first ever bottom 20 finish. What a joyous, beautiful and relaxed event.

When I finish, Adrian hands me my much-needed water bottle and leads me to what the boys have already discovered. Nearby, in the park, there's a misting shower where we all cool off. A misting shower, if you've never heard of such a thing, is a shower that sprays very fine water to refresh you and cool you down. You just walk underneath it for a quick spritz. We later come across some in Budapest too.

There's also a freezing natural stone paddling pool which is now full of parkrunners who have stripped off their running shoes and socks and are wincing in delight as the cold water soothes their toes.

We'd only had time for a light breakfast at the hotel so we have every excuse for hearty elevenses. There's a tranquil and enticing outdoor café and we order coffee, milkshakes, apple strudel and ice cream. We can't linger too long though as today is our main sightseeing day in Salzburg and we have a packed schedule ahead. Rory has devised a rather daunting "to do" list for today, our last in the city.

Hellbrunn Park is part of Hellbrunn Palace and Hellbrunn Palace is famous for its "trick" fountains which I have never heard of before but which I am now desperate to visit, especially as you get free entry with your Salzburg card.

Trick fountains, as their name suggests, trick you by lying innocently dormant and then springing into action and suddenly spraying you with water. This is exactly what we need right now with the scorching sun – and there are guides on hand to ensure you get just as wet as you want to. We want to! There's an informative audio tour explaining the background though we're more interested in getting splashed.

There's also a zoo here so after we've exhausted the fountains, we pay a quick visit. Most of the animals are hiding in the cool shade which is a shame but we can't blame them. I'd like to lie down under a shady tree myself but we have Salzburg cards and we need to use them! At least my favourites, the penguins, are out in force enjoying their pool.

Once we've caught the bus back to town, the next stop is a funicular up to the old fort. It's like a mini town up here with museums and a shop with interactive games. The views from the top are spectacular, with the city on one side and the mountains on the other.

There's loads to see including a marionette exhibition where you're instructed to open the door of a case. There's a skeleton inside and the camera flashes to catch your shocked face. Once outside, you can buy the photo. The boys look for ours and burst out laughing. The photos of them are good but I'm so small that all you can see of my shocked face is my hat and the very top of my glasses. "They should charge you half price for that" quips Kit.

We round things off with a stroll round more

squares, dinner – more schnitzel and stew – and a river cruise.

You know that last-night-of-holiday feeling when you feel desperately sad to leave, decide you'll definitely be back next year and gaze into the estate agent window to see if you can possibly afford to sell your house and move there? The problem with interrailing is that you get that very feeling over and over again.

And one place I am definitely not ready to leave is Salzburg. I could spend at least another week here, wandering over the many bridges, eating schnitzel and visiting the rest of the places on our Salzburg card.

We've adored it here. Three out of four of us have voted it "best destination so far", though Adrian's sticking loyally to Ghent. It's beautiful and serene and the food is wonderful. If only it could just have dialled the heating down a few degrees.

Tomorrow we're off to pastures new. I'm looking forward to more sightseeing, more beer...and a washing machine!

Steps: 36,644 (personal record and 25.2km); highest temperature 37C.

Discovery of the day: misting showers.

Day 9: Budapest

We do have to leave today, really we do, because we have an apartment booked in Budapest. It's a city I've always wanted to visit and we need time to explore that too. And it's a jolly good thing that Budapest is our next destination because otherwise I really don't think we could have torn ourselves away.

We're on the 9.07am train so after breakfast we make the short walk to the station and buy some sandwiches. It's a five-hour journey but the train is delayed. As we wait at the platform, I wonder whether fate is intervening to tell us we need to spend another day in Salzburg.

The train chugs lazily into the station – it's too hot for it to do anything else – and we hop on board. We're getting used to these long train journeys. First of all, you need to try to find somewhere nearby to store your luggage. Most trains have both overhead racks and big luggage areas at the ends of the carriage and sometimes in the middle too. Occasionally there is space between seats.

Before we set off, I'd been worried about our luggage getting stolen if we couldn't keep an eye on it. The first couple of days, when the train stopped at a station before ours, one of us would hover near to our cases to ensure no one removed them from the train without us noticing. But as time goes on, we've definitely become more relaxed. I occasionally glance out the window as people disembark and surprisingly not one of them is attempting to make off with our dirty laundry.

I can honestly say that except for the never-ending journey to Munich, I haven't once been bored on a train. I read my kindle, listen to an audio-book (though not nearly as many as I expected). I snooze. I research our next destination, where to go and how to get to where we are staying. If I've secured a precious window seat, I gaze at the passing scenery. I eavesdrop on other passengers' conversations though I can't understand most of them. Sometimes I even chat to my own family.

As we get off the train at Budapest, the heat hits us. It's a furnace. But first we need to do what we do at every station – find someone to take a photo of us under the sign which says the name of the place. Adrian started doing this in Belgium as he wants one of every destination for our photo book.

We have enjoyed varying degrees of success. The obvious problem with stations is that everyone is either rushing for a train or has just got off a train and wants to press on to their destination. It takes about 10 minutes to find someone here who isn't weighed down by luggage or children and doesn't look like they'll miss their connection if they pause to take a picture.

Once we've finally got the photo, we stroll through the station. If you ever find yourself in Budapest Keleti, do take a minute to look up and admire the graceful architecture. We spend a minute admiring the graceful architecture but mostly we are trying to work out where to get the metro from. We're not sure what ticket we need to buy so we go to the travel information centre. While we are waiting, I amuse myself by looking at the list of all the things you can do here, including paying a fine for fare dodging and complaining about a taxi. The latter sounds rather ominous. I assume from the fact it's specified on the "available here" list that it's a common issue and I'm glad we've vowed not to get a taxi throughout our trip.

We get the metro to "our" stop which involves a change of line. It's easy enough as there are only four of them. They are unimaginatively called M1, M2, M3 and M4. The metro itself is clean and fast and not too crowded. We arrive at Corvin-negyed and attempt to solve yet again the conundrum every tourist faces whenever they arrive at a new destination – which exit to take? This matters when it's boiling hot and you've got a wheelie you need to lug up the steps to get out of the station.

If I ever open a hotel, I am going to write the metro exit in very big letters on the website. And maybe email every guest too before they arrive.

Inevitably, we choose the wrong exit which adds a good five minutes to our journey and then, as we're walking on the wrong side of the road, we miss our side road. We're beginning to wilt, and sharp words are exchanged with the over-confident map reader. We're not in the scenic part of the city either – it's modern and rather nondescript, with a Greek restaurant and a large shopping centre en route.

We're staying at serviced apartments called the Escala Suites. This place was on my "treat" list of accommodation. Budapest hotels seem much cheaper than most of the places we are staying (apart from during the Grand Prix) but rather than cash in on that, I'd decided to trade up. We have a modern, stylish and spacious two-bedroom suite with a kitchen and lounge area as well as a balcony. There's a dishwasher, a hob and a much-needed washing machine. There are some interesting looking herbal teas, and breakfast is included too. All that's missing is a swimming pool.

They've left four large bottles of water waiting for us which we gulp back gratefully. After that, the priority is to get the washing machine on. I love the people who designed this studio as there is a massive airer to hang clothes on, which means we don't have to drape our pants in the shower.

We pore over the map to decide where to go to this afternoon. We opt to go back to the centre and walk by the Danube. We want to start our Budapest adventure with a cruise down the river but it's surprisingly hard to find where they start from. There's a lot of construction work going on and the place is very quiet. Where is everyone? Where are the boats?

In my arrogant British way, I'd assumed that because Hungarian is not widely spoken outside its own country, there would be signs in other languages (i.e English). But it turns out that this isn't necessarily true and we're having to use quite a lot of Google Translate.

We go to what we think is tourist information but they seem to be intent on selling us a Budapest Card. Unlike the fabled Salzburg card, this doesn't seem great value – at least for us, as we're not planning to visit many museums.

I'd always thought that Budapest would be one of the cheaper places to visit. This is seemingly confirmed by the great value hotel (which has worked out at £157 a night for the four of us including breakfast) and the cheap metro (about 80p a ticket). However when we search for somewhere to have dinner, the prices are on a par with Belgium. We have our first disappointing meal of the holiday. My chicken is nondescript and pretty small, which comes as a shock after the massive portions we've been served before. The currency makes it hard to work out the exact cost as there are something like 438 HUF (Hungarian forint) to the pound.

After dinner we wander back to the river and eventually find where the cruises leave. Boat tickets for the four of us are 20000 HUF or about £11.50 each. Unlike in most places, you don't book on a particular cruise. Instead, you just turn up when you fancy and join the queue. You might get on the boat or you may need to wait for the next one. We are quite relieved that we just fail to get on even though it means more waiting – the outside areas of the boat fill up quickly and late boarders end up having to sit inside. Not what we want on a gorgeous evening. As we're right at the head of the queue for the next, we plot where to sit. We hear others similarly hatching plans. It also seems that we're not the only ones surprised by the prices here. I overhear a woman saying, "I'm from Vienna and I can't believe that it's more expensive here than at home."

We eventually get on board the boat and take up a favoured position at the back, in the open. The timing is perfect as the sun is beginning to set and the river is beautiful.

There are seats around the edges and we have a great view until the middle section fills with people, making it hard to see anything. I wish we were on the benches in the main part of the boat. I stand up at one point to take a photo and someone cheekily nicks my seat. Another problem is that we can't hear the audio commentary so we mostly don't know what we are looking at. I say mostly as it's very obvious which one is the Parliament building. We've read it is modelled on the British Parliament so there's no mistaking it. It's dark now and it's lit up and twinkling.

At 11pm it's still 30 degrees and we're relieved to get back to our studio and the air-conditioning.

Steps: 19,960 (13.1km); how annoyed the two girls sitting

in our reserved train seats from Salzburg were when asked apologetically to move: very.

Most mocked holiday fashion item: my bucket hat. "I didn't know you were going to Glastonbury, Mum" said Rory innocently.

Day 10: Budapest

To the baths, to the baths! With a meltingly hot day in prospect, getting wet seems to be the most sensible thing to do. After much debate, we've opted to go to the Szechenyi baths as they sound the most fun. (Coming a close second is the Gellert baths which friends described as "like swimming in a cathedral".)

The Szechenyi baths are the ones you see on the front of every tourist guide, with a big outdoor area and people playing chess in the water. Or pretending to play chess while posing for Instagram photos.

I wake up early and while everyone else is sleeping I decide to book online. I really don't fancy a lengthy queue under a hot sun so I treat us to fast-track tickets.

Breakfast is included at our hotel and it's a help-yourself buffet with pastries, fruit, eggs, bread, mini sausages and just about anything else you could think of. You can sit indoors or on an outside terrace and it's a nice relaxing start to the day. I have three cups of coffee. We can go to the spa any time we like and it's a treat to be able to linger. We've done quite a lot of racing around and getting up for early trains so this makes a change.

First stop on the way to the metro is the shopping centre which is full of familiar names like Decathlon. The bath's website warns that it's compulsory to wear "slippers" by which we assume they mean flip-flops and I haven't brought any with me. (I do have some but inexplicably could only find one when I was packing. I'd lost half of a previous pair when I'd left them in the garden to dry, and a fox or a seagull made off with one of them. I don't think there's a fox or a seagull at the bottom of my wardrobe though, which makes it all the more mysterious.)

I buy the cheapest pair I can find for a princely 1400HUF – just over £3. They are a fetching pink which means that with luck they will be hard to lose.

We take the metro to the baths and discover that a) there's no queue after all, b) I have accidentally booked VIP tickets and c) the VIP entrance is several hundred metres in the opposite direction, which means I haven't made our lives easier at all.

Still, our posh tickets mean we have individual lockable cabins and we can change and leave our valuables there, which is much easier than finding a locker. It's all quite high-tech. Your cabin key is on a wristband and it doesn't show the number so even if you lose it, it's unlikely a would-be thief would successfully locate your cabin.

The baths, fed by natural hot springs, were built 110 years ago in 1913 and they are massive. They are ornate and echoey, with statues and mosaic murals. There are more than a dozen indoor pools all of different sizes and with varying temperatures – boiling, warm, tepid and freeeezing. There are also steam rooms and saunas which may be more tempting on a day when it isn't 38 degrees. The place is packed but somehow also manages to be calm and relaxing.

You leave your towel and slippers/flipflops/sliders on the side before gingerly lowering yourself into the pools. The boys dare each other into the icy pools four times. I manage it twice. They put their heads under. I don't.

The outdoor area is spectacular. We're used to icily cold lidos in this country, so it's a real shock to dip a toe into the pools and find them bath-hot. There are powerful water jets you can stand under for an invigorating neck massage. There's a queue for these but it's worth it.

The pools are great fun and there's one with a water current channel which whizzes you round at speed. I see a pair of sunglasses floating in front of me that have obviously been separated from their owner, so I grab them and put them on the side in the hope they'll be reunited.

Four hours later we emerge, relaxed of body and

soft of skin (the latter impresses some members of the party more than others).

Afterwards we follow our noses and find ourselves at nearby Heroes' Square. It's massive and there are plenty of very tall and imposing statues, but the square itself feels strangely empty. We really should read up about it in the guide book but not right now when the sun is blazing down. On one side, they are erecting a banner promoting the weekend's Grand Prix.

As we carry on wandering through the city, we find monuments round every corner. There are even statues of George Bush and Ronald Reagan.

We love Liberty Square with its many cafés and Budapest's own trick fountains. These are a little square of water jets that spring up and down at different times. Kit and I get briefly stuck in the middle as fountains dance around us, and we have to time our exit to avoid getting drenched. It's so hot that I am actually fairly disappointed not to get wet. However I'm a middle-aged woman and today I'm wearing a T-shirt dress so it really isn't an option.

I'd like to visit the Parliament building but again no one else seems keen. And I'm not keen either when I see the prices. Non-EU residents – that's us now – need to pay twice as much as EU members to do a tour.

Instead, we make our way to the nearby Shoes on the Danube memorial. It's really moving. Sixty pairs of shoes – a mixture of men's, women's and children's –

are old-fashioned, from a different time. They aren't real shoes; these are made of iron and set in concrete on the bank. They commemorate the Jews who were shot on the riverbank during the Second World War. As shoes were valuable, many were told to remove them before they were shot, their bodies falling into the river to be swept away. The shoes were often sold.

The memorial is simple and stark. Lest we forget.

We make our way thoughtfully back to the apartment via the supermarket (Aldi's if you're interested) where we buy pasta, sauce, juice, yoghurts and the finest Hungarian red wine (about £4.50 and entirely drinkable). We cook on the little hob and eat on the balcony, which is a bit of a tight squeeze.

For pudding, we polish off the last of the Bruges chocolate – how long ago that seems! It's the first time we've fully unpacked and it was a very pleasant surprise to find our little container full of marzipan at the bottom of the suitcase.

Steps: 18,007 (11.9km); number of washing loads done within 24 hours of arriving in Budapest: three; combined mozzie bite total: eight, with Rory contributing 0 ("that's because you're all bone," said Kit, affectionately.)

New family name for my beloved bucket hat: Mum's Muppet Hat.

Day 11: Budapest

I wake up early once more – this trip has done nothing to break that annoying 6am habit – and again I use the time judiciously. I find that you can download an app called Budapest Go and buy a daily group travelcard for 5000HUF – about £11.50. That's for trams, trains and buses for four of us, for 24 hours. London, take note!

This morning we use our travelcard to catch the bus to Memento Park, a few miles out of the city. It's here that they dumped the old Soviet statues after the fall of the iron curtain. A memorial to a fallen and disgraced regime, it's a weird place – in the middle of nowhere and, it feels, rather deliberately unkempt. "Look what you've done to us and where you've ended up!" it seems to whisper. The statues, which include the likes of Lenin and Marx, are massive. You can really see how intimidating they would once have been.

Particularly poignant is the replica of Stalin's boots. The original boots were once part of a huge statue of the cruel and powerful dictator. During the failed Hungarian Revolution of 1956, the statue was pulled down and hacked at until only the boots remained.

As well as the statues, there are little huts showing films about the intelligence services and secret agents and it's fascinating. We also see a photographic exhibition showing why the revolution failed and what the consequences were.

We'd planned to visit the House Of Terror Museum to learn more about the twin Nazi and Communist dictatorships which made the lives of so many so miserable for so long. But after this sombre but fascinating park, we think we need a change of mood and decide to leave it for another day.

We catch the bus back to the city centre and, in the sweltering heat, climb the steps to the Fisherman's Bastion high above the city. The views are stunning but the sun is intense.

Needing to get out of the heat, it's time for another museum. Wanting something entirely different and not remotely thought-provoking or sombre, we decide to go to the Museum of Illusions. Fabulous and huge fun with all sorts of optical illusions, it's highly interactive with enthusiastic staff on hand to explain how it all works and, most importantly, tell you where to position yourself to get the best photos.

There's one room where you can stand in a corner and look teeny tiny, and then move over to the other corner and appear to be a giant. For someone vertically challenged like me, this causes particular family merriment.

There's another illusion where you sit at a table and the clever mirrors make it seem as if there are at least eight of you. Kit sits there and I am genuinely unsure which one is the real him. It's probably the most unusual museum I've ever been to and I love it. We take a million photos. Well, perhaps 40.

Following our slightly meh dinner on our first night, I asked my new favourite Facebook Group Interrailing for the Older Crowd for advice on where to go to eat. They suggest the Jewish Quarter – of course! Why didn't I think of that?

It's a good thing we get to Mazel Tov restaurant early because although it's pretty spacious, practically all the tables are booked and when we leave a couple of hours later, there's a huge queue waiting patiently outside.

Mazel Tov is a riot of fairy lights and greenery and marvellous food. We have chicken thighs, spicy Moroccan sausage, pita bread, chips and dips. The place is rocking. Enormous portions in true Jewish mother style mean no one has room after we leave for chimney cake, the Hungarian speciality which is sold everywhere and which I have been eying up since we arrived. Still, there's always tomorrow.

We enjoy a stroll round the Jewish quarter including the Moorish-style synagogue which is the biggest in Europe. We can't go in as it's too late but it is wonderfully ornate and striking.

Steps: 23,226 (15.3km); number of statues in Memento Park: 41.

Funniest moment of the day: Kit's asked for proof he's a

student at the Museum of Illusions and conjures up a picture of
his A level exam timetable, which they are happy to accept.

Day 12: Budapest

We have a lovely chilled last day in Hungary, where the
temperature drops from scorching to merely very hot,
except when the sun comes out (which it doesn't
much).

After packing up and waving goodbye to our
gorgeous air-conditioned apartment, we climb the high
and steep Gellert Hill, which has a variety of steps,
paths and viewing points. Disappointingly, the very top
is roped off for renovation. You can buy an assortment
of items on the way including tablecloths and expensive
water. One is more immediately useful than the other.

Back down again, we take tram 2, "one of the top 10
tram journeys in the world" according to someone or
other, along the Danube. It's perfectly pleasant but we
think it's been a bit over-sold.

We go souvenir shopping, stopping at a café for
milkshakes and cake (pistachio and raspberry – as good
as it sounds.)

We've fitted in most of what we'd planned to do
here. We didn't get to Margaret Island and its lido
which is a shame, but we need something to return for.
Also, we never made it to the House of Terror, thinking

we'd done enough depressing Hungarian history for one trip. We've only been to one of the baths so we'll be back at some point to try out one of the many others.

We're off on our overnight train tonight so we decide to have a large, late lunch. We find a little local bistro for more beef stew and spend a couple of hours there, sitting at a table on the narrow pavement. It's the best and the cheapest meal we have in Budapest, probably because we are away from the main tourist area. Somehow, Kit finds room for chimney cake.

For the last time, and now very confident about which exit to take, we get the metro back to the Escala Suites where we've left our luggage. It's amazing how quickly you get used to, and slightly bored of, a particular route.

We're sorry to leave Budapest, especially as we've mastered the metro system, and loved our executive suite with free infusions (and a darn fine breakfast).

Steps: 24,653 (16.2km). Best star spotting moment: joining the crowds outside the Budapest InterContinental hotel waiting for someone, perhaps Max Verstappen, to arrive for the weekend's Grand Prix. We give up after 10 minutes.

Day 12/13: Sleeper train

There are few occasions in life when it's a positive advantage to be, well, rather a lot smaller than average.

Not when you're trying to reach the top shelf of the

supermarket, nor when you need to hang on to the ceiling strap on a bus and certainly not when you are struggling to see over the head of the person in front of you at the cinema.

However when you are in a cupboard-sized couchette on a sleeper train from Budapest to Zurich, you come into your own. It's a good thing we haven't brought a cat along because there certainly isn't room to swing it.

We arrive at the station ridiculously early (entirely my fault) for our 8.40pm train. On the plus side, there's certainly plenty of time to admire the architecture.

I'm clutching our all-to-easy-to-lose little paper reservation for our couchette, booked several months ago. Our train pulls in – I was hoping for a bright and modern sleeper but it looks rather old.

To get on the train, we have to give our reservation slip to the conductor who gravely takes it and then crosses us off a list. Paper and pen? It all feels wonderfully old fashioned. In fact it feels a bit like I've handed over my ticket to the school play.

In a night train, you usually book a seat, a couchette or a sleeper. Couchettes are little individual compartments with six beds in, three on each wall. You can only fit three people in a sleeper so that wasn't an option for us. I've read a description of a couchette as being a bit like a youth hostel on wheels and it's pretty apt. We've paid around £170 on top of our interrail ticket and it isn't exactly luxury.

Although couchettes sleep six, you can book it out for fewer people. We've done this as I didn't fancy sharing with a couple of random strangers and as it turns out I have no idea how they would have fitted in anyway.

In the carriage we find a little bottle of water and a strange chocolate each as well as a sheet and pillow – you have to make your bed up yourself. No frills here! If you're in a sleeper, I assume someone will do it for you. I think private sleepers have private facilities too. For us cheapos in the couchettes, the loo is at the end of the carriage.

There's a ladder at the end of the bed but it isn't attached to the top bunk and we're not entirely sure how to secure it. When the guard comes in, we ask him, and he stares at it with what seems comical bewilderment before finally showing us how it works. Then he returns to his task in hand – our breakfast order. Tea, coffee or juice? We've been promised a Viennese breakfast and we are all really looking forward to this.

The train was originally scheduled to arrive in Zurich at 8.20am but a few days ago OBB, the Austrian train company who I booked with, emailed to say it would be arriving two hours late, I think because of work on the track. This is disappointing to say the least because we only have one day in Switzerland and our time there is ever-diminishing.

We arrange luggage carefully under the beds and on the spare beds to maximise available floor space.

The compartment is so small there is really nothing else to do but lie on our beds and read. We take it in turns to go to the WC to brush our teeth. The boys are gone for ages. When it's my turn, I join a small queue outside. The person inside is taking so long I am not convinced there is anyone in there. I try the door but it's locked. Eventually, some full 15 minutes later, a young woman emerges. The next person goes in and takes a similar amount of time. Maybe there is some complicated spy activity going on and they are writing secret notes and hiding them in the cistern. We are in Eastern Europe after all.

Back in our room, I lie down and open my kindle. I haven't been expecting to get much sleep but the noise of the train is surprisingly soothing and I'm rocked to sleep by 10.30pm.

Day 13: Lausanne

We emerge unscathed from our claustrophobic couchette but with many questions about our night train experience.

– Why was everyone else taking so long in the WC? The same long wait happened this morning. It's not as though there is a shower in there – just a basin and a toilet. What is going on? Is my spy theory the right one?

– Why was everyone else on the train incredibly miserable, refusing to meet our eye or respond to a weak smile? Are they secret agents on a serious mission? Or tourists disappointed with the breakfast?

– I can understand the latter as our much-anticipated Viennese breakfast turned out to be what looks like a small soft pastry wrapped in white plastic. The tea was fruit tea with a mini carton of cream. Adrian poured it in before he'd realised this and it was completely undrinkable. None of us can face even opening whatever is in the white wrapper. Is this really what the city that invented Sacher torte has for breakfast?

– How on EARTH could you fit six people plus their luggage in a couchette compartment?

– Why did the police knock on the door at 7am, demand to know where we were from, shine their torch on the top bunk to see a dozing Kit and quickly depart?

– Why did they email us a few days ago to say the train would arrive two hours late when it arrived at the scheduled time? I'd woken up at about 7am, glanced at my phone to check the time and was greeted with a "Welcome to Switzerland. You can use your roaming pass while you are here" message from EE. We should not have been in Switzerland yet according to the amended timetable. I pulled the curtain and was greeted with an almost comically stereotypical view of a Swiss mountain. I asked the guard what time we'd be arriving and he gave me A Look and said "8.20" as though I really ought to know that.

And at pretty much 8.20 precisely, we pull into Zurich. The guard solemnly hands us back our paper reservation – I have no idea what I am supposed to do with it, but he obviously thinks we'd like it as some sort of keepsake – and helps us off the train with our luggage.

It means we can now make our original planned connection to Lausanne. In fact, our train is at the platform, seemingly waiting for us. Zurich station is gleaming and easy to navigate – you could learn a thing or two, Brussels! The train departs five minutes or so late. There are profuse apologies over the intercom so I gather this is a rarity in Switzerland.

Unlike the couchette, the train is luxurious, even in second class. The carriage is spacious and the seats are wide and comfortable. There is fabulous scenery round every corner. It's two hours to Lausanne and I am enjoying every minute. I could do with some breakfast though.

We get the metro to our hotel, which is another place I am nervous about. Hotel du Marché is extremely cheap for Switzerland. We've paid 180 Swiss Francs or under £160 for a quadruple room with a private bathroom.

It appears fine from the outside and the staff are helpful. Connecting to the hotel wi-fi is awkward but necessary given that most UK roaming packages don't include Switzerland (two of ours do, two don't). It's a complicated procedure to log on and they patiently explain the long-winded steps to do it.

Tourists are entitled to free public transport – that's part of the tourist tax you pay – and again it's all a bit complicated as we have to send an email to the hotel for them to activate it but they do this with good humour.

We're not expecting our room to be ready but they check with the cleaner and tell us she's nearly finished. For a budget hotel, their service is impeccable. The room, when we get there, is much more spacious than we are expecting and there's even a little kitchenette so we can leave water in the fridge. We'll forgive it for being on the fourth floor.

We still haven't managed any breakfast so we skip it and get lunch instead. We just want a sandwich and come across a supermarket with an amazing food hall. You can get rolls and pizzas and Japanese food and just about anything else you can imagine. It makes Waitrose seem like the local corner shop. The boys choose large pizza slices which staff heat up for them. We sit in the square and eat.

The main reason we have come here is to go to the Olympic Museum. Lausanne is Olympic HQ and I can easily see why they chose this location. The museum sits in a fantastic setting on the shores of Lake Geneva. It's perched on a hill and you can glimpse the lake and mountains through the trees.

The Olympic Museum traces the history of the Games and there is loads of memorabilia including Usain Bolt's shirt. There are mascot displays, an excellent section on women in athletics, and a history of the torch relays. I particularly enjoy the medal exhibition – I've always wondered what they look like close up. I'm also fascinated by the section on what it's like to stay in the athletes' village. I always thought it would be like a glorified university hall of residence, except with better food and fewer late night parties.

At the end there's an interactive section with games and you can even tune in to a mindfulness session.

I can't help wondering if they are going to mention the drugs scandals and they do – sort of. But it's more about how drugs tests are carried out. It all feels a little sanitised.

We pose for the obligatory photos on the winners' podium and have a sprint on the track section outside. For Olympic buffs like us, this museum is a must-see.

We've brought our swimming gear for a dip in Lake Geneva and aren't quite sure what to expect. But this being wonderfully-organised Switzerland, there's a dedicated swimming area near the museum, with a wooden deck complete with steps down into the lake. There's a fabulous view of the mountains and people of all ages are sunning themselves and jumping into the lake. The water itself is clear and cool but not cold. I live in Brighton but rarely dare to venture into the sea, mostly because I shudder at the thought of how dirty it is. This is my sort of wild swimming for sure (tame swimming).

If you asked me right now where I'd rather live, Lausanne or Salzburg, I don't think I could answer you. Maybe when I win the lottery, I'll buy a holiday home in each.

We'd thought about picnicking here but we fancy a proper meal now as we haven't had anything substantial since Budapest yesterday lunch time. We have repeatedly read that Switzerland is eye-wateringly expensive but I've done my research and found a small chain of burger restaurants called Holy Cow. The prices appear reasonable so we head off to the nearest one.

It feels a bit like GBK back home and there's a meal deal of burger, chips and a soft drink which you can upgrade to a beer for just a few francs. The burger is plump and delicious. Adrian says it's one of the best burgers he's ever had. The whole bill is 74 Swiss Francs or about £66. What a total bargain – and that's not something I ever expected to say in Switzerland.

Steps: 17,543 (11.6km).

Fact of the day: Lausanne is the smallest city in the world with its own metro (and it's so steep it feels like a funicular).

Day 14: Baden Baden

I wish we could have had longer in Switzerland especially now we've managed, thanks to careful planning and the Holy Cow, to escape with our bank balance intact. We have somehow spent less money here than on two of our days in Budapest.

Today we are repeating our three-countries-in-three days trick: (last week Belgium-Germany-Austria, this week Hungary-Switzerland-Germany). Our next destination is Baden-Baden on the edge of the Black Forest.

On the train from Lausanne to Bern, where we need to change, we get chatting to a local couple who are more than happy to tell us about the country and what it's like to live there. They tell us they won't visit London because it's so expensive. Given how pricey Switzerland is, this comes as a shock.

Switzerland is famous for being neutral so I am surprised when they reveal that Swiss boys have to do military service though they can do some sort of social service instead. Girls don't (yet) have to do it, which is apparently a bone of contention.

Language teaching is prioritised here and most people can speak French, English and German. The country is run by various committees made up of members of all parties and they all have to agree to support the chosen policy.

It's an expensive country because they pay people properly and protect the farmers, which makes food pricey. They're moving towards all food being organic, as well as becoming carbon neutral by 2050. Go Switzerland!

We have eight minutes to make our connection in Bern and this being Switzerland, I'm confident we'll make it which we do, comfortably. It's nearly two hours from there to Freiburg, where we change again for Baden-Baden. The platform is absolutely teeming with teenagers who swarm on to the train in huge numbers. They look like they are off to summer camp and I'm just relieved we are not on the same packed train.

Baden-Baden station is a few miles out of town so we need to get a bus. I have the address of where we are staying and know it is fairly central but the timetable on the bus stop offers up few clues. We go to the information office where they issue us with tickets and print out the time of the next bus and where we need to get off. It's three minutes by bus. I fear something has got lost in translation as I know we are about 5k away. We get off at the allotted stop and find we are nowhere near anywhere. We eventually work out we need to walk to another bus stop and pick up a second bus there.

It is pouring with rain and I am wishing we were back in Lausanne where everything was so straightforward, the sun was shining and I could understand the language.

When the second bus arrives, we aren't sure if the bus tickets are still valid or whether we need to buy new ones. Kit shows them to the driver who responds in a volley of German. We don't understand. "Do you speak English?" asks Kit. This is both the wrong thing to say and the wrong language to say it in. The driver looks apoplectic. We don't know exactly what he shouts in response, but we're pretty sure it's something along the lines of, "No I blooming well don't and you should speak German in Germany!"

I wave the tickets at him and ask "OK? (because OK is OK in German, isn't it? Maybe not). "Ja!" he shouts in exasperation. We slink past him and sit down, feeling pretty foolish. And also annoyed at ourselves because he's right: it is rude to assume people speak your language in their country. We mutter to ourselves that Rory, who's just taken GCSE German and can get by in the language, should have been at the front instead. Now all of us wish we were back in Lausanne.

A man behind us has seen what happened and is embarrassed – but by the bus driver, not by us. "I am afraid the driver was very rude," he says to us. "Is there anything I can help you with?"

Finding the apartment feels a bit like some sort of

Escape Room game. Navigate through town to the flats, locate the garage, open the safe box, plug in a code, get the key, find the right block, go up the lift, get out at the fourth floor (again!) go through the glass door and into the flat. We've got a two-bedroom apartment with a balcony and it's in a residential block for the first and only time on this trip.

The apartment is...furry. There are gloriously fluffy cushions on the stools and chairs. The beds have the thickest mattresses I have ever seen. Here, you don't fall into bed, you fall up to bed.

We are a little perplexed by the notice saying to be quiet between 9pm and 9am and also for a spell after lunch when everyone is clearly having a siesta.

We don raincoats for the short walk into town. The rain is easing and people are relaxing outside cafés. We sit down on one with a terrace and order – the waitress warns us that it is cash only. That seems to be very common here. We haven't brought many euros so straight afterwards we have to find a cashpoint to replenish them.

Baden-Baden is a graceful and stylish place. It shot to fame – in the UK at least – in 2006 when the wives and girlfriends (WAGS) of the England World Cup team stayed there. It has attractive parks and a concert hall. People stream past us, dressed up to the nines, obviously on their way there. There's a casino and loads of restaurants. It's more than a year since the Ukraine

War started and there is also some sort of protest about what we think is a Russian ballet dancer performing in town, with a counter-protest of others welcoming her. Police are hanging round good-naturedly and it's all very peaceful.

There is a statue of a gorilla in town but we're not sure why.

We have an unmemorable dinner, washed down with local beer, and head home to Apartment Furry. I debate whether using the tumble dryer after 9pm will contravene the "no noise" rule as I really don't want to upset the neighbours.

Steps: 18,820 (12.4km); number of times in a row we've been on the fourth floor: three; minutes on trains today: 225.

Day 15: Baden-Baden

Today is a healthy day. A day to reconvene with nature, swim at sunset, and not eat any schnitzel and chips. It's stopped raining, the sun is out and we don't have to get on any trains.

Baden-Baden is on the edge of the Black Forest and we've come here to enjoy the scenery. We've bought a map at the helpful tourist information office and have decided to go for the 9k "panoramic" hike, part of a longer route which was "twice voted the most beautiful walk in Germany". We really are suckers for that kind of accolade.

We've been to the supermarket again so we pack sandwiches and head off. The hardest bit seems to be finding the "start line" for the walk and we get lost a few times. The weather is perfect – about 23 degrees with hazy sunlight dappling through the trees. The route, once we find it, is pretty well signposted though we have a few inevitable "is it showing this way or that way?" moments. I'm surprised by how few other walkers there are.

It's cool and peaceful in the forest. There are viewing platforms with gorgeous views and the walking is easy and relaxing.

Our map has marked a café in the forest (and, most importantly for the middle-aged bladder, toilets!) The café turns out to be cash only so it's a relief we have some with us. Nearby is a ruined castle which is vertiginously high. It is aptly called Altes Schloss – Old Castle. The boys are delighted but I stay rooted to terra firma. They're up there for half an hour and report that the views are spectacular. "You'd have hated it," they reassure me cheerfully. They show me a picture they've taken of me standing at the bottom and even that makes my knees weaken.

With our café stop, lunch break and leisurely pace, the walk takes about four hours. It isn't a circular route but we can get the bus back. At the end there's a funicular – "the longest and steepest in Germany". You can walk up it if you'd rather, though I can't imagine how long that would take or who would be crazy enough to do it. At the top there are yet more spectacular views.

Back "home" we have a quick pasta dinner chez Apartment Furry and then we are off again – to the baths, to the baths! They're open until 10pm and we fancy a late-night swim to contrast to the heat-of-the-day Budapest one.

There are two thermal baths in Baden-Baden – one nude and one clothed. Well, swim-suited at least. Let's just say it's a good thing I've done my research beforehand because we'd all have been mortified if we'd turned up at the naturist one. Even in the clothed one, Caracalla, there's a big sauna and steam room area for those who prefer not to wear clothes.

The smiley cashier is delighted with Rory's attempt to speak German and gives him a short lesson in the language. She glances at the boys, turns to me, grins and says that she'll sell us tickets to the clothed areas only.

I ask where the women's changing rooms are and she responds with peals of laughter. "It's all mixed, welcome to Germany!"

The changing rooms are incredibly confusing. First, we have to find a locker, which is a bit complicated and has to be demonstrated by other helpful guests who are obviously used to bewildered tourists. Then there are the changing cabins themselves. We can't work them out at all. They open from both sides but there isn't a lock on either. We all change in our cabins as quickly as possible in a very British state of paranoia about someone coming in.

Just like in Budapest, there are both indoor and outdoor pools and here, you can swim between the two. Outdoors is landscaped with people lolling on sunbeds. There's a horse-shoe shaped whirlpool bath that is unbelievably strong – there's no way you can swim out of it when it's on so you have to wait for it to subside. There's also a water current channel which is enormous fun and you can't help getting swept up in it in every sense.

Inside are more pools of different temperature including the obligatory freezing cold one – I manage it twice.

The whole place is stunning, with a big glass dome over the main pool letting the late evening sunlight in.

Steps: 34,415 (22.7km); maximum incline of funicular: 54%; number of times they named Baden-Baden because it's so good: twice.

Day 16: Triberg

It's our last day in Germany and we enjoy a relaxing day trip to Triberg, an hour from Baden-Baden. We still have our L plates on when it comes to the buses. Today, we succeed in getting a direct bus to the station, but it goes all round the houses (and the industrial estates) before eventually dropping us off.

We also get the wrong ticket. The driver says (in German, obvs), "two adults and two kids?" when Rory tries to buy tickets and Rory thinks he says "there and back?" and says "ja".

We've already established that Rory and of course Kit need adult tickets here. I feel guilty the whole day. Well, maybe for the duration of the journey.

Triberg is known for three things: cuckoo clocks (which I always thought were Swiss), Black Forest gateau and a waterfall that's "the highest accessible waterfall in Germany." Or something.

The most important of these is, obviously, the cake, and we find a traditional looking café where we get a couple of slices. Black Forest gateau is much too exciting for our sons who just order chocolate cake, with Kit determined to prove he can eat a whole slice of Sacher torte himself.

The gateau, a tantalising mix of chocolate sponge, cream, cherries and kirsch, along with I dread to think how much sugar, is surprisingly light. Do I feel mildly tipsy afterwards or am I imagining it?

We walk off a few calories at the waterfall, a pleasant climb with good views and excellent photo ops. We take plenty, as well as some for other people, who take group shots for us in return. It is all very convivial. It takes about an hour to go up and down and in an attempt to get you to stay longer in Triberg, entry to the waterfall also gives you free admission to three nearby museums.

The best thing about the Black Forest Museum is the section on cuckoo clocks – and not for the reason you'd imagine. Some wag has scrubbed out the letter L in every "clock" treating readers of the English version to a solemn explanation of the history of cocks in Germany.

Apparently Triberg also has the world's biggest cuckoo clock, but it's a couple of miles away and we decide we can live without it. There is a myriad of cuckoo clock shops in town, of course, with shop staff wearing traditional German outfits. Some of the clocks cost thousands of euros. We make do with a cuckoo clock fridge magnet.

Our last stop is the Fantasy Museum. It's designed for Instagrammers rather than oldies like Adrian and me but we love it. You can take ridiculous photos (look, there's Rory bursting out of a cuckoo clock, oh and here's me popping my head out of a slice of Black Forest gateau). It's hilarious and we take numerous photos.

We're aware that there's only one train an hour back to Baden-Baden but we don't want to know when as that will probably mean rushing. Inevitably we miss one by about three minutes. I see the next train is to "Uhr" at 16.03. When I look up a few minutes later, I see it's been delayed to 16:07. This goes on for quite some time before I realise "uhr" is German for "time". I've been looking at the digital station clock. I really do need to learn a few words of German before I come again.

We'd planned to cook in tonight but there aren't any supermarkets open and frankly we can't be bothered. Instead we go to a beer garden. We have a lovely, relaxing meal and quite a lot of beer, followed by a stroll. It's a beautiful summer's evening and everyone is sitting outside the town's many cafes, having a beer or an ice-cream or both. We have both.

Back at Apartment Furry, we're frantically trying to get our washing dry. It's well after the 9pm deadline but surely a quick blow of the tumble dryer is OK? I have no idea how loud the machine is, how well insulated the apartments are or how tolerant the people in the flat below are. We risk it – after all, we'll be out of here in the morning – but don't manage to get everything dry.

Meanwhile, we're packing up with more thought than usual. We've only got one night at our next destination and we try to put everything we need for that in a single bag, to avoid having to open the others. We designate three cases as Bags That Must Not Be Opened.

Steps: 21,562 (14.2km); fridge magnets bought: three; time alarm set for tomorrow: 6:30am.

Day 17: Baden-Baden to Utrecht

We steal out of Apartment Furry at 7.30am, hoping our squeaky suitcase wheel doesn't infringe the "no noise before 9am" rule. If anyone does tut at us, they do so from behind closed curtains and we escape without being ticked off.

We catch a single, speedy bus to the station. Rory asks for the tickets in German and I swear the driver almost smiles at us. We've finally mastered Baden-Baden. What a shame we're leaving.

The station is heaving. There are kids everywhere, backpacks laden, looking like they're off to school which is a bit baffling. It's late July: is it back to school time already for German kids, or have they not broken up yet?

We have breakfast at the station café which has a massive choice of pastries, breads and coffee – and some sort of weird and unhealthy pizza pastry I pretend not to notice the boys eating.

Today's journey means going via Düsseldorf. With a 90 minute connection time, it's great not to have to rush for the next train. We find appetising sandwiches at the station (with a Dunkin' Donut for the boys), get fleeced a euro each to go to the toilet and dodge the worrying number of beggars.

Today's destination is Utrecht which was, to be honest, a bit of an afterthought. Plan A had been to spend one night in Paris. I'd got as far as booking a hotel and even looking for somewhere to eat. But we changed our minds when we realised how expensive the seat reservations would be if we wanted to get there by fast train. Instead, we thought we might as well race straight to the Netherlands and give ourselves an extra day there.

Utrecht is a bit of a transport hub and, more importantly, looked cute and appealing, so it won our vote. It scored extra points for a very cheap night's accommodation. We've booked a private room in the Stayokay youth hostel for 114 euros including breakfast. (We get a discount for early booking and another for being YHA members).

The station is bright and modern – I'm not sure what I was expecting, but it wasn't that. The minute we emerge, I regret the fact that I am wearing shorts. It's not freezing but after the warmth of the last week, the comparison is stark. My jeans are in The Case That Must Not Be Opened Tonight but at least we have our raincoats to hand.

Stayokay is about 10 minutes' trundle with our cases from the bustling station and it's a very cheery place. Inevitably, they've given us a room on the fourth floor, but the staff are smiley, there's a spacious café/restaurant and the place is buzzing so we'll forgive them for that.

We're enthusiastic youth hostellers back home and

it's been a while since we've had to make up our own bed at hostels. But Utrecht obviously didn't get the memo so we dutifully tuck in sheets and shake down duvet covers. It's harder for the boys, who are in the top bunks. I claim to be too small to reach up and help.

How sweet is Utrecht? The answer is very. There are canals below street level, with precarious steps down to restaurants beside them. And there are, of course, cyclists everywhere, sometimes two to a bike.

We have dinner at a department-store-turned-restaurant called Winkel van Sinkel – we choose it mostly because we like the name. I have a beer with an unpronounceable name which the waitress says is so rude she doesn't want to translate it. It also has a robot taking away dirty plates, the first time we've ever seen such a thing.

Last week, when we were baking in Budapest, I looked with envy at temperatures in Holland. Last night, we were sitting outdoors in Baden-Baden at 9pm eating ice cream. This evening, it's grey and chilly and we spend an hour sitting inside the Stayokay café drinking hot chocolate to warm up. This is hot chocolate with a difference, though. They serve you a glass of hot milk and your choice of white, milk or dark chocolate buttons which you pour in to melt (keeping one or two back to nibble). It's board games evening so we play a couple of rounds for wholesome family entertainment before heading off to bed on the fourth floor.

Steps: 17,121 (11.3km); train miles travelled: 440 approx; windmills spotted: one.

Fact of the day: this is Holland's biggest university city with 70,000 students, according to the mural in our room.

Day 18: Utrecht to Delft

Our room has a fantastic view of the square below and Adrian spends 10 minutes, forehead pressed to window, staring outside. Is he taking in the atmosphere, perhaps, or deciding where to go for elevenses? Neither – he's determined to keep looking until he finds a single cyclist wearing shorts rather than jeans. And he triumphantly spots two, meaning it's clearly not too cold for him to wear shorts too.

My jeans, meanwhile, have been retrieved from The Case That Must Not Be Opened, which is opened and quickly shut again. Everybody notices but pretends not to.

After breakfast – a tempting buffet of bread, fruit, cake and cereal – we go in search of the free walking tour.

I've learnt my lesson from Munich and have already booked it to make sure we get on it this time. The confirmation email tells us to look out for the tall Dutchman or woman with the white umbrella in front of the Dom Tower. Puzzlingly, we eventually find an average-sized woman and it is a good thing it isn't raining yet because when it does later, every single person seems to have a white umbrella.

The Dom Tower is apparently Utrecht's most famous monument. I'd never heard of it till yesterday, but now I am unfathomably annoyed to find it is covered in cladding. It's part of a five-year restoration project due to finish next year. Our guide, an art teacher, says she reckons they'll have to start re-restoring it as soon as it's finished.

Our walking tour confirms we'd actually seen most of central Utrecht's major sights last night.

We do, however, learn about the one and only Dutch pope – to our delight called Pope Adrian – who donned his robes in 1522. It took several days for the news of his election to filter through to Adrian, who wasn't best pleased to say the least. Adrian didn't want to be pope; he wanted to retire to his big house in Utrecht and no-one else seems to have wanted him to be pope either. When he died a year later, there were apparently three days of celebrations. There's a suitably modest statue of him in the centre.

There's also a statue of Miffy, a Big Deal in Utrecht as creator Dick Bruna lived here. There's a Miffy Museum and even a special Miffy traffic light.

I want to get a picture with Miffy – who wouldn't – but some children are playing near the statue and it takes ages for them to move so that we can get a quick snap. Honestly! It's as if Miffy was designed for kids! My own teenagers are non-plussed. "Who's Miffy?" they ask.

For lunch, we want to eat somewhere local, rather than a chain, and spend ages deciding where to go. Eventually we choose a café called Bagels and Beans (the beans they refer to are coffee rather than baked/green/broad).

Afterwards we jump on a train to Delft, which somehow manages to be even cuter than Utrecht (and it sounds better too as I can't help thinking Utrecht sounds like a urinary infection).

This is our final move and I've booked us a family room in an olde worlde hotel right beside a canal. We are – for the first time since Brussels – on the ground floor. There's a bit of an embarrassing start when we can't open the door and have to go back to reception to get help. The nice receptionist manages it instantly. It just needs a bit of welly.

There's a double bed in the room, and a couple of chairs, and a telly. But where are the other beds? We open a door – oops, that's the bathroom. And another one – nope, wardrobe. We hunt fruitlessly for a pull-down bed, and, ridiculously, a false wall. We go on to the patio outside and search for another door.

Defeated, we return to reception. After failing to

open the door, we're a bit embarrassed to have to go back and admit we can't find all the beds either.

We think they'll accompany us back to our room, point to two more beds and say chirpily, "Look they were here all along!" before going back to the staff room and laughing about those idiotic Brits. Instead, they come with us to the room and solemnly agree that yes, there are four of us but only beds for two. They had managed somehow to book the family room twice over and the other family have beaten us to it. What a c(l)ock up!

They put two extra beds in the room and promise to speak to the manager about some sort of discount. The spacious room is now decidedly cramped. Meanwhile we head off for a beer and a stroll in a lively square crammed with bars and restaurants.

Delft is magnificent. The main square, Markt, is massive. There's an imposing church at one end and a glimmering town hall (Stadhuis Delft) at the other. There are cheese shops and pottery shops and ice-cream parlours and cafés and everything else you need. One disappointment though is when we spy another Bagels and Beans – Google later informs us there are more than 70 in the Netherlands so the independent café we thought we'd lunched in earlier was clearly anything but. After this, we seem to spot them everywhere we go.

For dinner, we settle on a fabulous little place called

Boterhuis which brews its own beer. I pair it with a scrumptious chicken satay. Delft is delightful and delicious, and we're definitely glad we came.

Steps: 21,455 (14.2km); number of staff trying to sort out the bed conundrum: three; time The Case That Must Not Be Opened was opened to retrieve jeans: 8am.

Facts of the day: 50% of journeys in Utrecht are made by bike and the city is home to the world's largest bike parking area, with more than 12,000 spaces.

Day 19: Amsterdam

The hotel redeems itself somewhat this morning with an excellent breakfast. There's freshly squeezed orange juice, loads of fruit and pastries, fruit loaf and a pancake machine that works when you wave at it. It's all served on delicate Delft china. Adrian is particularly happy to get a full teapot of tea, though he is bemused by the lack of milk jugs and ends up pouring milk into his tea from a bowl.

We don't have much time to enjoy it though as we're off to Amsterdam for the day. One of the reasons we chose Delft was because it meant we could stay somewhere where we could easily commute to Amsterdam while avoiding its sky-high hotel prices (though maybe they'd have given us enough beds...)

This, annoyingly, is scuppered by engineering works, which I'd noticed a couple of days ago when looking at train times on the app. We double checked with the ticket office at the station when we arrived who confirmed that there were replacement buses for the next couple of days. The woman there advised us to allow more time than expected to get anywhere. "The drivers will probably get lost," she'd explained. "That's because they're from Utrecht."

We have a bit of a ticking clock today because we have a timed ticket for the Van Gogh museum – 10.30am with stern warnings to arrive within 30 minutes of our allocated slot. I am very keen not to be late. We booked tickets back in February when I happened to look at the website and saw there were only limited tickets left for the dates we were going. It would be maddening to lose it because of the replacement bus.

I'm not sure whether the driver is from Utrecht or not but luckily he does know the way. The bus drops us off at The Hague and we then search for the train to Amsterdam. There are two stations we can go to – one, Amsterdam-Zuid is 20 minutes' walk to the museum but there's one ready to depart for Amsterdam Centraal, 40 minutes from the museum ("a more interesting walk" Kit has promised). We jump on that one.

It's a bit of a stressful walk to the museum and 40 minutes seems a bit optimistic especially as we get lost a couple of times. I can see those Sunflowers wilting and vanishing in front of my eyes. There's no time to stop and admire the canals as we march onwards, past the Rijksmuseum and its queue, arriving at Van Gogh with precisely nine minutes to spare. There's no queue here, possibly because of the "sold out for today" sign outside.

The museum is airy, light and seems so modern that I'm surprised to learn it's been open for 50 years. That means it must have been here last time I came, back in 1988, but I don't remember it. Here you can find lots of insight into Van Gogh's life, his mentors, his friends and his mental health. There are many paintings by his contemporaries too.

I like the way the museum is so self-aware and on the wall are comments from art critics and others about the way the paintings are laid out. One questions whether Sunflowers should be on a separate wall – apparently when the museum opened it was just hung with the others. Does doing this create a hierarchy, effectively saying one painting is better or more significant than another? Should one delicate painting be behind a screen or does that affect our viewing of it? Is there any point to art if you can't see it?

There are a few glaring omissions, though, and there's definitely a big Starry Night-shaped hole. (It lives in New York.) I have to stifle a giggle when I see a tour guide showing her group a picture of it on her iPad. It's as close as they can get to it.

The museum encourages visitors to sketch some of the paintings and the boys – not known for their artistic prowess – decide to give it a go. Rory draws Kit and Kit draws one of Van Gogh's self-portraits. Let's just say neither will be gracing a gallery wall any time soon.

After getting away with only spending a few euros on a fridge magnet in the shop, we leave the museum to wander the streets and gaze at the canals. We haven't bought tickets for the Anne Frank house but it would be interesting to see it from the outside so we head over there.

I went to the House when I was nine during a trip with my parents. I remember going in the front door but now there's a glassy entrance round the corner, complete with shop and cafe. On the door itself there is now a simple plaque and tourists pose beside it, many grinning and with thumbs up. It all feels a bit wrong.

Amsterdam feels a bit off too. Perhaps it's because we're a bit jaded, perhaps we've seen too many canals, but we just aren't wowed by the city. It feels like Utrecht and Delft's older, uglier and seedier big brother. It's dirty, teeming with tourists and just a bit unlovable.

When we find we've accidentally wandered back to the train station, we're a bit relieved. The train stops at The Hague and we make a snap decision to get off and have a quick look round. We amble through the streets rather than making for any sights as we've done enough for today and it's getting late. We make it as far as a café most memorable for its very steep stairs up to the loo. I decide I haven't had enough ice cream this holiday so I stop at the parlour next door. I'm usually a pistachio or mint choc chip woman but the chocolate ice cream looks so dark and inviting that I opt for that. Its flavour is deep and rich.

Back in Delft, we eat spare ribs outside a pub with a wonderfully friendly waitress. We tell her we've been to Amsterdam and are delighted to be back in sweet, pretty Delft. "I hear that a lot," she says.

Steps: 33,129 (21.8km); number of paintings produced by Van Gogh in his final 70 days, 74; number of bikes pulled out of Amsterdam's canals each year: 15,000.

Silence from hotel on possible refund for room shenanigans: deafening.

Day 20: Rotterdam

A week or two ago – in Salzburg maybe, or Budapest, or perhaps Lausanne – Rory glanced up from his phone and said, "I don't suppose we are anywhere near Rotterdam on our last Thursday, are we?"

I replied that yes, we were, and a smile lit up his face. He'd been studying the pre-season friendly list of Dutch champions Feyenoord, who are based in Rotterdam just a few minutes from Delft.

We're a family of football fans, with Adrian and Kit supporting Brighton, and Rory and I fans of Watford (I know, I know – and you don't need to make any jokes because I have heard them all before.)

Not only did it mean we could go to a match, but it wasn't just any match. Feyenoord was the new home of ex-Brighton player Ali Jahanbakhsh, who will live long in the hearts of Seagulls fans for a spectacular goal – an incredible overhead kick which rescued a point against Chelsea. Despite an otherwise rather underwhelming stint at Brighton, he is known fondly (in my house at least) as the Iranian Messi.

And in this match, Feyenoord's opponents are Spanish team Villarreal – home of former Watford midfield maestro Etienne Capoue.

Getting tickets to see our former heroes in action was no mean feat. I handed responsibility to Kit who decided to put everything in my name. First I was registered on the Feyenoord website which meant I could now buy tickets. Or so we thought. When we tried to actually purchase them, my card kept getting rejected.

There was a number you could WhatsApp the ticket office on, but only once you were in the Netherlands so guess what practically the first thing we did when we arrived on Dutch soil was?

I wasn't convinced that this would work but we sent them a nice message explaining we were holidaying here and would love to see Ali J etc etc. They got back pretty much instantly and within minutes the tickets were ours.

We decide that we should spend the whole day in Rotterdam and then go to the match in the evening. It means another trip on the rail replacement bus, but we are getting good at it now. The problem is that today we have to endure the worst weather we have experienced the whole trip and the rain is pelting down.

The architecture is amazing and we cross a famous bridge, Erasmusbrug, also known as The Swan, which is apparently the heaviest bridge of its type in Western Europe. We're so soaked through by this point that our heavy jeans and rain-drenched jackets no doubt add a few more pounds. The rain is lashing down, visibility is poor and we make it three quarters of the way across its 800 metre length before giving up. We spend about half an hour in a tourist shop choosing a fridge magnet just to keep out of the rain.

Rotterdam has a huge indoor food market with loads of stalls so we go there to dry off, removing soaking coats the minute we get inside in an attempt to get them dry.

My eyes are out on stalks. There are so many places to eat that we spend a good half an hour trying to decide. We consider Greek, Japanese, duck burgers and noodles before settling on various types of chicken curry all round.

When you can peel your eyes away from the food, you have to admire the building which is another architectural marvel. It's a massive arch with the walls and ceiling a kind of mural. (It's been described as "Rotterdam's very own Sistine Chapel" which might be pushing it a bit.) There are also apartments – how incredibly tempting it must be if you live here to nip down for some churros every evening. The residents must have iron willpower and/ or a wardrobe full of trousers with elasticated waists.

After our curry, we prowl round again, looking for pudding. We are again spoilt for choice. There's cheese and chocolate and ice cream and nuts and so much more. The boys choose stroopwafels while Adrian and I settle on cannoli, little pastries with a filling of your choice. Adrian opts for hazelnut and I go for my favourite pistachio. It's tiny but so rich I struggle to finish it.

By now the rain has finally stopped and we take the opportunity to visit the Cube Houses which Rotterdam is famous for. These are cube-shaped houses tilted at an angle of 45 degrees, as a way of maximising space. One is even a (Stayokay) youth hostel. We go inside one and the slanted windows make me feel a little queasy.

And so it's time for the match. We join the throng at the station heading to the stadium's own station.

Feyenoord fans are known for their passion and here they are on the platform, singing at the top of their voices. I keep having to remind myself that it's only a pre-season friendly.

In the ground, the atmosphere is amazing. Everyone is drinking beer and to our astonishment, smoking, which was outlawed in British grounds decades ago. The singing doesn't let up and some of the songs are a surprise too. There are Feyenoord versions of "Daisy, Daisy give me your answer do," and "Sweet Caroline". It isn't exactly difficult to pick up the words and join in. Our stand sings to the other stands which reply in song too.

The game itself is full of passion. There are even a couple of minor altercations. A not so friendly friendly. Capoue scores a screamer for Villarreal – I swear I never saw him do that for Watford – and Ali J equalises for Feyenoord from the penalty spot. What are the chances, eh?

The ground erupts when Ali scores, with plastic beer glasses thrown in the air in jubilation. We duck as we've finally dried out and don't want to get soaked again. Afterwards, I expect it to take ages to get away from the stadium as everyone seems to be heading to the same train. But shuttle trains whisk us away back to the city centre in minutes.

Finding our way to the bus replacement to take us back to Delft isn't so easy. It's late and there are no station staff around. We join a small international committee trying to work out where to catch it from. Global co-operation triumphs.

And so back to the hotel which has been firmly in the doghouse since 4:06 this morning.

That's the exact time an ear-splitting fire alarm erupted, waking us abruptly from our sleep. Blearily, we grabbed clothes and joined the pack in the corridor by the front door. No one wanted to go outside as it was pouring.

Two things quickly became obvious: there was no fire and there were no staff on site. No one was quite sure what to do.

There was a frisson of excitement when the fire brigade arrived a few minutes later. "If I was five years old, this would have been my dream," quipped Kit, a former Fireman Sam fan, as burly firemen filed into the building. Most guests were standing with fingers in ears, trying to drown out the ear-splitting alarm.

After strolling through the hotel, one of the firemen made an announcement. It was in Dutch so I couldn't understand it but it went on a bit and no one moved so I deduced he wasn't saying, "there's no fire so you can all go back to bed."

I asked a fellow guest for a translation. "He said, 'there's no fire but the hotel was sold recently and they don't have the new owner's contact details so they

can't get the code to turn off the ear-splitting alarm,'"
she said helpfully.

About half an hour later a man arrived with a key,
opened the alarm and switched it off. There was a small
ripple of applause and everyone trundled off to bed.

This doesn't do much to improve my impression of
the hotel. When no one got back to us about the room
mix up, I sent an email pointing out that we had
booked a family room but were squashed in a double
room with camp beds for our sons. Given we didn't get
what we had paid for, could we please discuss a partial
refund?

I felt this was entirely reasonable but the hotel
seemed to disagree. They said we could now switch to a
family room (literally too late as we wouldn't be back
till 11pm tonight and only had one more night after
that). However, they went on to say everything was
fine. We had booked a suite and we had been given a
suite! (This to me was a bit like saying, "You ordered
fish and chips for four and you've got fish and chips for
two! You ordered fish and chips and you got fish and
chips! Tell us – what's your problem exactly?)

However, they did come up with one more very kind
and considerate offer – a 20% discount on our next stay
if we booked directly. We declined.

*Steps: 22,761 (15km); number of songs we know about
Rotterdam: one; attendance at match: 30,000.*

Question of the day: just who did set the fire alarm off at 4am?

Day 21: Delft

The subject of the curious incident of the fire alarm that went off in the night is not mentioned by the hotel staff at breakfast, which is a quiet and subdued affair this morning.

Luckily, we have a quiet day planned. Although we've been in Delft for three nights, we haven't seen much of the place yet – during the day at least. We haven't yet been to the porcelain museum, which seems a bit rude given that it's what Delft is best known for. So Adrian and I wander off there this morning while our had-enough-of-museums sons try to find where parkrun is instead.

The receptionist at the museum is a lovely young Scottish guy who greets us like old friends and excitedly says, "I've had half the UK here this morning."

It's an interesting museum which tells the story of the pottery; it seems they nicked the idea from China. I really like the commemorative plates including one celebrating the signing of the Treaty of Versailles. "Pax" it says with what turned out to be undue optimism – we all know how long that lasted.

We're allowed to see the workshop with painters

and potters hard at work. They are studies in concentration. I wonder if anyone has ever shouted "boo!" and made them drop something.

We emerge into the world's most expensive gift shop. I pick up a tea towel for my mum, who loves Delft, but put it back quickly when I see the €51 price tag.

We do have a nice coffee though, served in Delft cups of course, in the idyllic garden our Scottish friend has begged us not to miss.

Afterwards, we reunite with the boys and decide it's time to add to our growing list of Dutch towns. We nip to Leiden, 20 minutes away, for a chilled afternoon of more canals and coffee. It's a really nice place but canals aren't as exciting as they were when we first arrived. I do get a lovely picture of a windmill surrounded by flowers. Sadly it isn't open today so we have to admire it from outside.

Leiden is the birthplace of Rembrandt and there's a really unusual and striking tribute to him here – young Rembrandt standing gazing at a bronze self-portrait of himself in later years. There's also Leiden Castle to explore. Built on an artificial hill, you can walk along the top (so unscary even I manage it) and take in the views.

We have coffee (not in Bagels and Beans) in a cute café before we go back to the train station. We get a sweet little biscuit with it.

It's our last night tonight so when we get back to Delft – thankfully no replacement bus service to get confused about today – we decide we'll find somewhere special to eat that we can come back to later on. We come across a little Greek restaurant on a stationary barge. When we return a couple of hours later, it takes us ages to find it. There are so many canals and corners in Delft and many look the same.

Delft is buzzing tonight. The bars are crammed and there's a Chamber Music festival in the main square. It's such a beautiful, charming, idyllic and relaxing place.

Steps: 28,283 (18.6km); number of times Kit has been ID'd this holiday when ordering beer: 1 (tonight); relationship with hotel: stalemate.

Day 22: The final day

It's time to celebrate the last day of our holiday the best way we know – with a parkrun. Sadly Kit, who has been hobbling a bit for the last few days, decides he's not up to a vigorous 5k and stays behind.

Lurking in the Delft suburbs, the parkrun was set up and run by a Londoner now living in Delft with his Dutch wife. It's a two-lap course, which gives Rory less chance of lapping me though I still wouldn't put it past him. It takes in woodland and a lake and reflects Delft itself – it's small, charming and extremely scenic. With 33 runners this week, it's even tinier than the Salzburg version – and thankfully a lot less hot. What a difference a fortnight and 600-odd miles makes!

Delftse Hout parkrun is just 7km from the one in The Hague and therein lies its problem. The Hague's parkrun is called Zuiderpark. The observant among you will notice that it starts with the letter Z and therefore it exerts a hypnotic pull over parkrunners trying to complete the "parkrun alphabet." Zuiderpark has exactly 100 more runners than Delft today, even though I am assured (and I completely believe) that this one is much prettier.

Unfortunately, we can't stay around for post-run coffee and cake as we need to go back to the hotel to check out. As we are clicking shut the final case, I see an email from them, finally offering us a €40 refund, the difference between the two rooms. It isn't much but it doesn't really matter now and we can (and obviously do) go straight off to spend it on coffee and some really rather excellent cheesecake.

A couple of days ago, we'd spotted some inefficient kayakers paddling straight into the bank on one of Delft's little canals and the boys decided they wanted to show them how it's done. So they go off to try to hire one while we go to the Vermeer exhibition. This is less exciting than it sounds as although the celebrated but enigmatic painter was born here and lived in Delft all of his life, none of his paintings are on display here in his hometown.

New York has snaffled most of them and even his most famous work, Girl with a Pearl Earring, is down the road in The Hague. What's here are reproductions and information about what they do know about him, as well as his technique.

There's a nice gift shop where I pass up the opportunity to buy a single pearl earring (just €19.90).

The boys message us to say they haven't managed to kayak as they couldn't find anyone at the boathouse. They come to find us outside the exhibition centre where we take it in turns to stick our heads through a cut-out of the Girl with a Pearl Earring. There's just time for one last lunch, one last beer (two actually) and one last photo of us eating before we need to start the long journey home.

We pick up our cases from the hotel and wend our way to Rotterdam for the Eurostar. Unlike St Pancras on the way in, the terminal here is an oasis of calm. There's plenty of room to sit as we wait for the train.

Sadly we are going to have to finish our journey by coach rather than train because there's a train strike. I'd been checking the National Rail app all week, which showed most trains were running. Until last night that is, when everything after about 7pm had a big red "cancelled" sign next to it.

When the strike was announced a few weeks ago, I

immediately swooped in and bought us coach tickets before they all sold out/ went up in price so we would have a way of getting home. Just as well as it turns out.

Our Eurostar arrives early, well before 8pm, but our coach is not leaving until 10pm.

We get the tube from St Pancras to Victoria, which is deserted, and kill an hour in the restaurant area. Adrian and I aren't hungry but the boys inevitably are and polish off huge wraps.

Then we trudge to the coach station and pick up the coach home to Brighton from there. If we'd caught the train, we could have been home in an hour but the coach takes a long route down to the south coast via both Heathrow and Gatwick airports. At least I manage to nab a window seat.

It's a real shame to be ending our epic train adventure on the road, but it has a nice symmetry to my first interrail trip in 1988. Back then, in those pre-Eurostar days, our ferry from Belgium ran aground and we were so late arriving there were no trains so they had to lay on buses.

That journey was hilarious as there was an A Cappella group on the ferry who were returning from a competition. To cheer the bored passengers up, they sang "I'm on top of the world," to warm applause. So they sang it again. And again. And again. And about 20 more times. Sometimes I sing it to my travel companion Hil, still a great friend, to remember the good old days.

Steps: 29,105 (20.4km); estimated time of arrival home in Brighton: 12:45am. Apologies in advance to sleeping locals for the annoying suitcase-with-the-squeaky-wheel.

The day after

We stumbled through our front door at 1:01am. Since then it's been raining non-stop (not ideal when you've got four cases of washing), my computer has thrown a tantrum (and so have I) and I somehow managed to get stung by a bee that had sauntered into the neck of my jumper while I was sitting at my desk catching up with several hundred emails. Welcome home, eh?

We loved almost everywhere we visited, and we had some great experiences – the Feyenoord match, the mountain coaster (not me, obvs), the Black Forest hike, the trick fountains in Salzburg, singing along to The Sound of Music tracks, the parkruns, the Budapest baths, the strudel, the beer...

I go into battle to try to get a refund for our cancelled train home. Southern Rail tell us we're probably not entitled to compensation for our long journey back because a) they aren't sure they can offer compensation for interrail tickets and b) they amended the timetable (i.e. cancelled the trains) and therefore we can't claim for services that weren't scheduled to run. Go figure.

When I point out that there certainly were trains scheduled to run when we bought our interrail tickets, they reply telling us to get in touch with customer relations who will review on a case-by-case basis. This sounds like a lot of effort for a probable "no".

I just want to cover the cost of our coach tickets so instead I contact Interrail who do give us a rebate for lack of trains. It seems a bit mean of them to have to cough up though. Still they'll get it back again as I immediately put it in next year's holiday fund.

Yes, next year's holiday fund. We've already decided that we couldn't imagine going back to a holiday where we laze around the pool, just putting down our books to pop into the buffet and load our plates with a strange combination of food (I have a picture of a much-younger Kit with a fried egg, pizza, pasta and broccoli).

I've already caught myself leafing through the Train Travel in Europe guide once more. We have talked about Innsbruck and Interlaken, Lake Bled and Luxembourg. You never know – maybe next time we really will make it to Croatia. There's one thing I'm definitely going to do before we go: buy a tin of WD40 for the suitcase with the squeaky wheel.

Overview

Modes of transport: 10 – train (obvs), bus, minibus, coach, metro, tram, boat, funicular, mountain slider, chair lift.

Cars and taxis: 0 (smug face).

Total steps: 540,737; distance walked: 358.4km (222 miles); distance travelled by train: 4752km (2,953 miles); time on train: 2 days, 2 hours, 9 minutes.

Different beds: 10. Favourite: the world's deepest mattress in Baden-Baden. Least favourite: moving bunk bed on the sleeper train.

Most beautiful place – a dead heat between Salzburg and Lausanne. We wish we'd had longer in each.

Best family activity: fridge magnet hunting. I stole this idea from another interrailer. It was great because it really made us think about which image summed up a place for us. As a bonus, it gave us something to do when it was raining. Now I remember our trip every time I get out the milk.

Fridge magnets bought: 16. Fridge magnets that we

couldn't find for seven weeks until it turned up in the secret pocket of my daypack: 1 (Budapest).

Best museum: impossible choice between Memento Park and the Illusion museum, both in Budapest. Oh and then there was the Olympic museum. And the Van Gogh. No, I give up.

Most moving: Shoes on the Danube, Last Post at Menin Gate.

The why can't we do it as well back home question: city squares, little biscuits with coffee (and no I'm not talking about the ones that come in plastic wrappers), double-decker trains, beef stew, chocolate, talking to tourists in their own language.

Chapter 3
Interrailing in 1988: The Manager or the Rats

"The manager or the rats, you're bound to wake up with one of them." So proclaimed the graffiti scrawled on the peeling wallpaper of our Paris hotel on the first night of my virgin interrail trip back in 1988. I was 20 years old, not terribly streetwise, and a trip across Europe was by far the most exciting thing I had ever done. There were four of us – two old school pals, Hil and Amelia, and a university friend, Julia.

What I most remember about that first interrail trip was the heady sense of total freedom. I still recall staring up at the departure board in Paris, and seeing trains departing for Milan, Antwerp and Zurich. "We could go ANYWHERE" I thought.

Part of that freedom was the lack of contact with anyone back home. No-one knew where we were. There were of course no mobile phones, no text messages or Facebook posts. There was no point sending postcards as we'd be in the next-country-but-one by the time they arrived.

We'd agreed with our parents that one of us would ring home from a phone box (remember those?) once a week to tell them where we were and reassure them that we were still alive. The chosen parent would then ring round to the others. When it was my turn, I took particular delight in announcing "We're in Munich" as my parents were under the firm impression we were in Greece.

While the essence of interrailing is the same as back then, so much has changed. In the 80s, just about every interrailer had a large rucksack – I don't think wheelie cases had been invented or if they had, I couldn't afford one. My rucksack was weighed down with books. I was an avid reader and was terrified of running out of reading matter. How I'd have loved a kindle. I also took my precious Walkman and a few CDs rather than the Spotify app and audio books which I listened to more than 35 years later.

I've got a lovely glossy photobook as a memento of our 2023 holiday but my 1988 version is rather different: an old-fashioned photo album. I'd posted off my rolls of film to Bonusprint in a "freepost" envelope together with a cheque, and waited impatiently for them to arrive back through my letterbox. I always told myself the holiday wasn't over until I'd seen my photos. Once I'd discarded the blurry ones, I stuck the rest in an album. Alongside, typed laboriously on a manual typewriter, are my short diary entries.

The first photo in my album shows us setting off from Victoria station. Nowadays, interrailers mostly get the Eurostar to mainland Europe, but back then there was the train-boat-train (or as I kept calling it, to everyone's confusion, the boat-train-boat – I'm not sure where we would have ended up with that). You'd get the train from Victoria to Dover, then the ferry to Calais, and from there pick up another train to Paris. It took so long, you couldn't really get much further than France on the first night.

In Paris we stayed at a cheap-and-nasty-hotel which I've never forgotten the name of. It doesn't seem fair to mention it by name as Google shows me it has transformed itself into a 3-star hotel, with a "superb" rating on booking.com.

Back then, however, it was a grimy, old-fashioned affair with decades-old wallpaper and a bidet in the middle of the room. You even had to pay extra for a shower.

Diary entry: 4 September 1988

"The graffiti in the room of our "hotel" made us giggle and certainly it proved a rather inauspicious start. On the verge of falling down and in need of rather a good lick of paint, it also

boasted a rather shady manager who refused (correctly) to believe that only one person had used the bathroom and that he was not being "done" out of his 12F for a shower."

Our next stop after Paris was Verona in Italy. We got a night train and the carriages were pretty much the same as today.

Diary entry: 7 September 1988

"It was 14 hours from Paris to Verona and we decided it would be more painless to make the journey overnight. Accordingly, we booked a couchette. Question – how do you get four solid lumps of girl, four heavy rucksacks and hand luggage into a couchette about the size of an airing cupboard in the pitch black without waking the two innocent lads already asleep in there? The answer is you don't, but they were very obliging about the whole thing. Their considerate behaviour was sadly not matched by the guard who insisted on returning passports and reclaiming sheet sleeping bags at 7.30am, coupled with a request to "se lever" immediately. Still, this was to provide good training for some of the more sadistic youth hostels that we were to encounter later."

I'd completely forgotten what it was like before the establishment of the border-free *Schengen* area, when every time you crossed a border, the train would screech to a halt and guards would come on to check your passport. Sometimes staff would take these off you on night trains so that border guards didn't need to wake you up at 3am. Sometimes they didn't.

Diary entry: 9 September 1988

"When we arrived in Verona, we got on a bus to the youth hostel but had no idea where to get off, so we played our first game of 'follow the rucksack'. These rucksacks, like so many we were to encounter, belonged to a group of Australians. Australians seem to take a year off work and travel the world in that time. THEY certainly seemed to have the transport system sussed.

"The youth hostel, as it turned out, was thoughtfully situated at the top of a hill, just perfect when it's the middle of the day, scorching hot, and you're carrying a heavy rucksack. Still, it was well worth the climb and we were cheerfully greeted by friendly staff. The price of 10,000 lira a night included breakfast AND showers, and dinner was only 7000 lira – which included wine!

"Verona itself proved to be quiet and beautiful, if not particularly exciting. They milked the Romeo and Juliet theme for everything they could, and there was even "Juliet's tomb" to visit which rather puzzled me."

Ah, lira, not euros! What a problem money was for the interrailer of the eighties. Not just running out of it, which we did, but changing it into different currencies and using up our last pennies/ cents before we got the next train to a different country. As a student, I didn't have a credit card and I don't think debit cards had arrived on the scene either. What I did have was travellers' cheques, so every time we arrived in a different country, we immediately had to find somewhere to exchange them for cash.

Diary entry: 10 September 1988

"The first thing you see when you come out of Venice station is a canal – it must be the most fantastic setting for a train station anywhere. The (fairly) early sunshine glistens on the water as people mill about. Our trusty bible Europe by Train advised us to take water bus number five to the youth hostel, so we obediently did so."

Just about every interrailer had a copy of Europe by Train, which, in those pre-internet days, told you where to go, what to eat and where to stay. My now dog-eared copy is a fascinating reminder of how much things have changed.

Europe was of course divided back then, with many countries behind what was known as the Iron Curtain. Poland seemed a particularly difficult place to go to – according to Europe by Train it was almost impossible to make an unplanned visit. You needed to organise it all beforehand and write off for student accommodation vouchers.

It's also incredible to look back on some of the rules. How different things were. The book warned that in Belgium, hoteliers could be imprisoned for up to three years if they allowed unmarried couples under the age of 21 to sleep together. It seems unbelievable that this was a Western country less than four decades ago.

Anyway, back to Venice, where it appears that the setting of the youth hostel was fabulous but the ambience was anything but.

Diary entry: 11 September 1988

"Venice youth hostel is sparkling clean but run rather like an army camp. A master switch snapped all the lights OFF at 11.30pm sharp and ON again at 7.15am, accompanied by the ringing of bells and the playing of the radio at full blast over the intercom. 'It is absolutely impossible to leave before 7.30am' barked the notice at reception.

"Still, a youth hostel is really only somewhere to sleep and it wasn't such a hardship to be woken so early in the morning when you could look out of the window and see the splendours of Venice.

"All roads seem to lead to St Mark's Square, which was crammed with tourists. We took a stroll round the back streets in a determined attempt to find the 'real' Venice where Venetians live and were amply rewarded. Tiny streets are

divided by the smaller canals and houses overlook the water. Washing hangs precariously over the canals. The sun beats down and Venice seems the most peaceful, the most beautiful place on earth.

"Venice I shall always remember; for the take-away pizza and the mosquitoes as well as for the boats and bridges, the gondolas and the Bridge of Sighs, the hordes of people and the exorbitant prices."

* * *

From Venice, we headed south to Florence where we failed to get a spot in the youth hostel. Back then, unless you wanted to phone all your planned hotels/ hostels in advance, which no one ever did, you had to turn up and hope there was space.

Most youth hostels shut during the day, so you'd have to join the lengthening queue outside. Like many British bed and breakfast establishments at the time, which would gleefully throw you out after breakfast, they seemed to be run for the convenience of their staff rather than their guests.

In Florence, as in several other places, word filtered down the queue that they had run out of space for the night. So we had to hoist our rucksacks on to our weary backs and return to the train station. Hotels would employ people to greet backpackers and persuade them to stay at their establishments. "Pensione?" they'd cry.

"How many people are you?" We'd haggle about the cost and whether it included breakfast before following them back. Some of these places were a bargain – many weren't. At least with a youth hostel, you knew pretty much what you'd be getting and how much it would cost.

We lucked out in Florence though, ending up with a spacious room and a good breakfast. Food features heavily in my diary.

Diary entry: 14 September 1988

"Florentine ice-cream is supposed to be the best in the world and we found the shop that supposedly sold the best in town. It was incredible. The whole trip was worth it just for a taste of their chocolate mousse ice cream!"

Diary entry: 16 September 1988

And so to Rome.

"After the artistic tranquillity of Florence, Rome was a bit of a culture shock. A friend had recommended a pensione near the Trevi Fountain. Bus 492, she said. There seemed to be about 100 different buses outside the station and it took us at least half an hour to locate 492. Still, we climbed aboard and sat happily for about 15 minutes before we realised that we did not

have a clue where we were going. Somebody had the bright idea of looking at the map and we discovered that, rather predictably, we were going in completely the wrong direction.

"For several minutes we comforted ourselves with the thought that it was probably a circular route. However, the driver put an end to that by unkindly driving up to the bus station and turning off the engine. He was rather surprised to turn round and discover four confused-looking young women on the back seat. Luckily, he found the fact that we had got the right bus going in the wrong direction hysterically funny and personally supervised our getting on the right bus, instructing the driver to tell us where to get off. Needless to say, the pensione was full so after all that we headed back to the station and engaged the services of Arthur "Chef de Pensiones" to find us a room. The hotel cost 22,000 lira a night (stale rolls and cockroaches no extra charge.)"

Diary entry: 17 September 1988

"Modern Rome is dirty, noisy and chaotic, populated by several million people who appear to loathe tourists. Their chief delight seems to be in making everything as incomprehensible as possible. Even buying a slice of pizza is confusing: do you get a ticket and then queue up for your pizza? Do you pay first or last? Is it all self-service? All this is heightened by the locals' charming habit of completely ignoring you if you are doing something wrong.

"Still, all this is made fairly bearable by the young Italian men, most of whom, we accidentally discovered, seem to congregate in McDonald's after dark.

"Nearly as stunning was papal Rome. We were so overcome by St Peter's that we spent three hours there. Neither was the Sistine Chapel a disappointment. The ceiling was being cleaned and the colours were beautiful."

Amelia, who was Catholic, wanted to say confession in St Peter's. She hadn't been to church since we'd been away and was apprehensive of being told off by a stern priest. Instead, he wanted to hear about where she'd been to on the trip. "Don't worry about it," he told her cheerfully from the "English spoken here" booth. "Enjoy your travels and go to church when you get back."

We made a big decision in Rome. Our initial plan had been to carry on going south. We intended to go down to Naples before catching a ferry to Corfu and on to Athens. But interrailers we met on the way were full of tales about the horrendously long journey back from Greece on trains with baking carriages and blocked toilets. I was rapidly going off the idea, and so was Hil, who was struggling with the heat. After much discussion in Rome, Hil and I decided to turn round and head north, to Germany, Switzerland and the Netherlands. while the other two stuck to the original plan.

We'd had a blast and a lifetime of shared experiences so it was an emotional parting. Today we'd have been constantly WhatsApping the other two to see how they were, where they were, and whether their pensione included breakfast, but of course we had no way of knowing. "I wonder what they are doing today?" we'd ask ourselves frequently. I think that as they were going to cheaper countries, they eked their money out for longer than we did.

Diary entry: 18 September 1988

"We celebrated our last night before splitting up with a bottle of vodka and a bop at the local disco. At first, the number of men (50 approx) to the number of girls (four – us) led me to suspect that it was a gay club. However the looks we received soon made me change my mind."

* * *

Hil and I caught the overnight train from Rome to Basel – and this time, joyously, we had a couchette to ourselves.

Diary entry: 20 September 1988

"Basel station, when we arrived at 10am, could not have provided a bigger contrast to Rome – it was sparkling clean and well organised. We stopped at the station buffet for a hot chocolate and pastry which, contrary to what we had been led

to believe, was very reasonably priced. The Information Office was very surprised when we asked the way to the youth hostel. "Follow the signs, of course." The youth hostel was clean, well-situated and cheapish, with good, generous meals – two cups of coffee or chocolate and orange juice for breakfast. Such luxury.

"Both Basel, which we wandered around that afternoon and Lucerne, which we visited the next day after Europe by Train advised that it was the prettiest town in Switzerland, were full of the most helpful, polite people, all of whom seemed to speak impeccable English. Everything was so well organised, so calm and so tidy – everything that Switzerland is supposed to be."

After Basel, we went to Munich and the now infamous youth hostel. We didn't much like it at the time but I'm actually glad we stayed there – Hil and I still howl with laughter about it today.

I can't remember where it was but according to my diary we got a taxi there, which probably contributed to our rapidly draining funds.

Diary entry: 21 September 1988

"You are welcomed (I think that should be in inverted commas) to Munich youth hostel by fetching green iron bars outside the hostel and an unsmiling man sitting behind a screen at reception. The whole place is covered in graffiti. We are sent to

the fifth floor (Block C). The showers are in the basement (Block A).

"Still, we got a good night's sleep until 7am when a voice boomed over the loud speaker telling us to get up. This was repeated in increasingly agitated tones every five minutes. We eventually obeyed and dragged ourselves downstairs. A man was sitting behind a desk, carrying out random checks on the queue to make sure we all had tickets and no one had come from another part of town, got up at 6.30am, forced their way between the iron bars, strolled past the guy at reception and gate-crashed breakfast."

Things didn't seem much better once we'd left the confines of the youth hostel – we were shouted at in the ticket office and denied access to a beer garden toilet because we were the equivalent of 2.5p short of change.

Diary entry: 23 September 1988

"Munich itself is an attractive place. However, to our shame we failed to go to the Oktoberfest, partly because neither of us really like beer. We met plenty who did go, though; most of them also seemed to be catching the 1.23am train to Amsterdam."

* * *

Diary entry: 24 September 1988

"Amsterdam, our last and wettest port of call."

Unfortunately, I'd failed to pack a raincoat, partly because we had planned to go to hotter climes and partly because I'd refused as a point of principle to listen to my mother. As it was pouring, I needed to go and buy one and I remember going to the Dutch equivalent of Woolworths to purchase the cheapest one I could find.

As a rather smaller-than-average person, I could buy a children's one – a kindermac – even more cheaply.

"My kindermac was a lovely red shiny thing of which I grew inordinately fond. It fitted quite well apart from the fact it was obviously designed for a kinder with rather short arms and a huge head.

"Like proper tourists we saw the Rembrandt paintings, took a canal trip, ate lots of chocolate, watched the buskers in Dam Square and wandered (unintentionally) into the red-light district. I like to think we oozed style in all these places, but somehow, I think our attempt failed."

Hil and I interrailed again the following year, this time to Spain and Portugal. My diary got as far as noting that it took 36 hours to get to Madrid (maybe we accidentally got the boat-train-boat instead of the train-boat-train?) I started my first job as a journalist just after we returned home, so I suspect that by the time the photos arrived in the post I didn't have the time, energy or inclination to do my "photo book." I know we went to Barcelona, Seville, Cordoba and Granada as well as Lisbon and the Algarve. But although I have a few photos in an album, I can't remember much about it at all.

Did I take my kindermac? Did we stay in any particularly inhospitable youth hostels? My memory is all but blank.

I'm hoping that recording every last detail of this latest trip means we'll never forget the finer details of interrailing 2023 edition. I am hoping that it has inspired in my sons a life-long love of travel, especially by train. My fervent wish is that this book will motivate other middle-aged people, or those with kids, to give up their flight to the continent and comfortable hotel, grab a map of Europe and take an interrail trip instead.

I can't wait to do it again – see you in the buffet car?

Interrail then and now

Then: travellers' cheques
Now: Apple Pay
Then: language dictionary
Now: Google Translate
Then: lira, pesetas, francs, escudos
Now: mostly euros
Then: Thomas Cook European Rail Timetable
Now: check train times on the app
Then: Three rolls of 36-exposure film
Now: hundreds of phone photos and videos
Then: Europe by Train
Now: websites and Trip Advisor
Then: postcards
Now: Facebook posts

Chapter 4
On the Right Track: Helpful Hints and Tips for Interrailers

Packing and baggage: to wheelie or not?

On all the interrail Facebook groups, the most contentious question isn't where to go but what type of luggage should you take? The choice is between a wheelie suitcase and a traditional rucksack.

There are those who swear by a backpack. The advantages are many – it leaves your hands free, making it easier to hold a map/ your phone/ a child's hand. A backpack is easy to carry up and down station stairs, and you don't risk a wheel falling off in a cobbled street, which according to travel forums happens more often than you might expect.

Wheelie fans counter that their luggage choice is much easier. There's no weight to carry and they are better for those who may have bad backs or not-so-young hips.

We decided to go for wheelies, partly because we had plenty of them already and only one backpack, which the kids had used for Duke of Edinburgh Award camping trips. All of the cases we had were pretty small – the kind of thing you take on a weekend break or as cabin baggage on a flight in the days when a small case was free – so we invested in one more slightly larger one. I was hoping we'd get away with three but it was too much of a squash so we ended up taking one each.

We didn't regret our choice. They were easy to manoeuvre and as we didn't overpack, they weren't too heavy. This meant we could carry them up a few steps where we had to. We found them easy to store on trains too.

Being able to open them up fully meant it was much easier to find things than rummaging round the bottom of a rucksack. We only completely unpacked a couple of times. One tip though – wheel an old case round the block before you go to check the wheels are still running smoothly. Oh and that they don't squeak!

My biggest new discovery was packing cubes. I'd never heard of these this time last year but once you begin reading reviews, you start to think you can't possibly manage without them. People describe them as life-changing. I think that's going a bit far but they did come in pretty useful.

Packing cubes are effectively pouches of different sizes that you use to separate items in your luggage. They usually come in sets and you can get all sorts of different sizes. If you want to go the whole hog, you can even buy ones that compress to save you even more space in your case.

I chose a basic set of seven for under £10. We put our swimming suits/ trunks, towels and hats in one which saved us a lot of time searching through cases when we went for our first swim. Adrian had another one for running gear.

My set came with a laundry bag which was ideal for stashing dirty socks etc. between washes.

The most useful one of all was probably a largish pouch which we designated the electricals bag. On every previous holiday, phone and kindle chargers started off in the pocket of someone's case before inevitably getting gathered up and put in a different bag which meant we were constantly searching for them. Into the pouch went power banks, adaptors and chargers, so everything we needed was firmly in one place. This was particularly important as we were constantly packing up and moving on.

The cubes took on different purposes as the trip wore on. They were especially useful to separate dirty clothes from clean as the washing built up. I repurposed one for fridge magnets as my collection grew.

As well as the wheelies, we took a small rucksack each as a day bag, though we didn't all take them out every day in practice. In here we kept essentials like water and waterproofs, plus books when we were on the train.

I splashed out on a new brightly coloured backpack with a few pockets to make finding items like suncream easier, but everyone else made do with existing backpacks. They all had outside pockets for water bottles which is pretty important when you are walking around all day in the heat (and saved cash too as water was very expensive in some places).

We decided to take a lightweight cold bag and some ice blocks with us so we could make ourselves a packed lunch. We barely used this, partly because we kept forgetting to put the ice blocks in the freezer, or, more often, didn't have a freezer. We wouldn't bother with this again.

Finally, I wanted to invest in a really secure little bag to keep valuables safe. I'd read too many stories of pickpockets before we went, especially at train stations. And we were visiting a LOT of train stations and were very obviously tourists.

One story that always stuck in my mind was about someone who put their hand in their bag when they were on the metro somewhere in Europe only to discover someone else's hand was already there. The thief removed their hand and the pair just stood and stared at each other until, to everyone's relief, the train arrived at the next stop.

After much debate, I bought a little crossbody bag from a company called Pacsafe who specialise in anti-theft bags and luggage. (Other brands are available – I also read good things about Travelon). My Pacsafe has an anti-slash design and two lockable compartments. I mainly used the front one for things like sunglasses and a charger so never bothered to lock it.

The second compartment held items I really didn't want to lose – credit card, phone, keys and everyone's passports. I didn't like carrying passports everywhere but in theory your interrail ticket is not valid without it. (In reality no one ever checked.) I was also mindful that they double as ID which you need to carry at all times in many countries.

I appreciate that no bag is completely thief-proof and if anyone really wants your bag they will get it, but this made me feel much more secure. Unlocking it was a bit of a fiddle (which to be fair is exactly the point) so I didn't always bother to fasten it. The bag sat at my hip so I could place my arm over it, and as it was in front of me it meant it wasn't easy for anyone to open even if it wasn't locked.

As it turned out, we never felt threatened the whole trip but this really gave me good peace of mind, especially at the start. Adrian wore a money belt which he got heartily sick of, especially in the heat.

Verdict: There really is no right answer to the case or backpack debate. Go with what you feel comfortable with, or what you already have in the loft. Just make sure you don't take anything too huge. We saw quite a few people dragging massive fortnight-holiday style cases. These blocked aisles in trains and they were really awkward to heave up and down those station stairs. Some trains (looking at you, Belgium) do have steep steps, so bear that in mind and make sure you can lift your case on.

I would recommend packing cubes for a few items. They were handy and inexpensive. I can't imagine travelling anywhere without the electricals bag again.

What we packed

Once you have selected your luggage, the next question is what to put in it. If you join one of the Facebook groups, you will see some examples of highly competitive packing – tiny backpacks with owners announcing triumphantly that this is how much they are taking for three months. I imagine they must have got very bored of their T-shirts.

We packed as if for a one-week holiday and planned to wash en route. Do factor in time to get clothes dry! (We left Baden-Baden with several damp items of clothing.) Many youth hostels also have washing facilities and if not, you'll just have to find a launderette.

What you pack is of course personal but here are some useful things I took with us:

Our **microfibre towels** were invaluable. These little towels are light and quick drying. We needed them for the baths and also for one of the youth hostels – we would have had to pay to rent some otherwise.

We packed a **small medical kit** with headache pills, antiseptic cream and plasters. We also took mosquito repellent, suncream and after sun.

Neck pillows – Adrian and Kit used these constantly and although they are a bit bulky, they were pleased they took them as they do make long journeys more comfortable.

Washing sheets. A pack of these are about the size of a pack of wet wipes. You just add one or two to a machine load and you can use them for handwashing too. They are really effective and take up no room whatsoever in your luggage. It means you don't have to hope there is some detergent in your apartment, or buy an unnecessarily large pack of powder when you arrive.

We took five **phone chargers** (a good idea as one of them stopped working in Austria) and **three power banks**. One was an existing, super-powerful Anker charger which can charge two phones at once. It's brilliant and really quick, but rather heavy. Before the trip, I invested in another, lighter Anker charger to carry around with me on day trips. Adrian also brought along his little iWALK charger which I'd bought for his last birthday. It's small enough to put in your pocket or running belt and I thought it would be useful if he ever ran out of "juice" when on a long run, especially as he uses his phone constantly to check his blood sugar. Turns out it's also perfect for an interrail trip. Three power banks might sound like overkill but it meant one was always fully charged and we didn't risk running out of power. Mobile phones are now essential on this type of holiday. You need them for Google Maps, for finding somewhere to eat and for entertainment like listening to podcasts. We had mobile tickets so these were also on the phone.

We brought along **two multi-adaptors**. These have four slots so can charge four phones at once when you are in your room. The plugs themselves are interchangeable – we use the British one at home so just slotted in the European adaptor to take away with us. Having two was good so they could be kept in different rooms. As well as phones we had air pods and a kindle with us so there were always things to recharge.

Adaptor for Switzerland. This country uses a different plug which I was aware of before we went. I spent about £6 investing in a two-pack UK to Switzerland adaptor.

We also brought a **reusable insulated water bottle**

each – don't leave home without these. These kept water cool in hot weather. We filled up every morning before we left wherever we were staying and it meant we only had to buy water in a few places. I have a loathing of single use plastic water bottles, which are terrible for the environment and tend to be really expensive. (In desperation on a boiling hot day in Salzburg I ended up spending about €3 on a tiny bottle.) We also filled them up from free water fountains which were available in quite a few places.

I took a few **freezer bags** which were good for sandwiches and could be reused, along with two **small plastic containers**. We used these for everything from an opened bar of chocolate to keeping parkrun wrist bands together. I also brought along a **small reusable carrier bag** which folded up into itself. This was useful for when we went to the supermarket.

The interrail ticket. Have you toggled yet?

When I went interrailing in the 1980s, your ticket was a little paper booklet which you filled in every time you got on a train. You can still get a paper ticket today but there is now also a mobile option.

Paper versus mobile is another debate that rages on the interrail forums.

Lots of people, particularly those of a certain age, seem to worry about how tricky the mobile version is to use. I won't give you a step-by-step guide (that's on the Interrail website if you need it) but you basically create a trip on the Rail Planner app and connect it to your pass using the number you were emailed when you bought it.

You can add as many train journeys as you like – the train you're planning to take plus the one before and a later one, for example. Just before you board the train, you press the little toggle bar beside the correct journey to activate it. If your train is late or you change your mind, you can untoggle it and add a different journey. "Have you toggled yet?" became a familiar refrain on our trip.

You then go into the "show ticket" section of your pass and at the start of every day it creates a new QR code. This is effectively your ticket each day and you show it to anyone wanting to check your ticket. It's also what you need for automatic ticket barriers to get in or out of stations.

One note of caution: we did read of people getting fined if they hadn't toggled their train as strictly speaking, they were travelling without a ticket.

It sounds a bit complicated but you soon get used to it. The biggest issue we had – and one that seems fairly common – is when the app stubbornly insists "no ticket yet today" despite the fact you have obediently added and toggled your journey. The answer to this is to put your phone into airplane mode and try again. We had a few panicky moments when we couldn't get it to work, especially in the Netherlands when you need to scan your ticket to get in or out of the barriers. This was massively annoying when we were sprinting for a train. It did eventually work every time.

If you want to avoid all of this and you're not keen on technology, you can still get a paper ticket. There are advantages to this as you don't have to worry about your phone running out of power or the app glitching at the crucial moment.

There are also disadvantages though. You have to physically write each journey on, which means crossing things out when you end up on a different train due to delays or whatever. Delays or whatever seem to happen quite a lot on European trains during the summer peak.

If you lose your paper ticket it's gone and you'll need to buy a new one, whereas you can transfer a mobile ticket to a different phone. The biggest disadvantage of all, I think, is that when you buy a paper ticket you need to specify the start date. We bought our mobile tickets in the 10% off sale before we knew our dates so this was the decider for us.

I've talked about the interrail ticket as if there is only one option, but there are many. Interrail tickets come in many different guises.

The main things to decide are:

- Do you want a continuous pass or one where you travel on a set number of days? A continuous pass means that your ticket is valid every day during that period – so buy a 22 day ticket and it will be valid for the whole time. The alternative will give you a number of travel days within a particular period (e.g. four travel days within one month or 15 days within two months). These can be cost-effective if you are planning to stay a few days in each place. If you are making a lot of day trips, it may be worth buying a "five days within one month" type ticket and using your pass for long journeys, paying for local trips on the day.
- How long do you want to go for? There are continuous pass options from 15 days to three months.
- Do you want a global pass that allows you into a large number of countries, or would you prefer one that permits you to travel within just one? The global pass (it should really be called a Europe pass!) gives you access to 33 European countries including Lithuania, Denmark, Serbia, Poland, Greece

and Croatia. You can buy passes for, for example, five days in a month in Italy or 10 days in a row in Germany. These could be best for you if you want to spend most of your time in one country. Of course, you could string several of these together to explore a number of countries.

- Do you want to travel first or second class? First class offers more comfort and you're more likely to get a seat if the train is packed. There can be other benefits as in some countries you can relax in the splendour of first class lounges at stations. I thought the second class one would offer more of a traditional interrail experience and of course it was cheaper.

- Children aged 11 and under are free, and those aged 12-27 can buy a youth pass which is a little cheaper. There is also a reduced rate for over 60s.

- One other thing to ask yourself is – is it actually worth getting an interrail pass or should you just pay for individual journeys? This is a bit of an unanswerable question and you'll need to price it up yourself. Some advance journeys can be great value but they are restrictive. Some rock-up-on-the-day fares are eye-watering. Of course, fares also vary considerably from country to country. I started to do the maths on our trip and pretty soon decided that a continuous pass was the best value, especially given the flexibility it offered. We bought the 22 day pass. Interrail has sales once or twice a year so look out for those as you can typically save 10%. You can sign up to their mailing list to make sure you don't miss them.

- There are a few rules – you can't use interrail within your own country, though you do get an outward and inward travel day. This meant we got "free" travel from our home station in Brighton to St Pancras to catch our Eurostar. And in theory from St Pancras back to Brighton at the end, though that didn't work out. Speaking of Eurostar, you can take advantage of a special reduced passholder fare. These are limited in number and do sell out at peak times so once you know your plans, book it.

- Finally if you are wondering whether you can still use interrail now we have left the EU, the answer is a resounding yes – we're still European. There's also a Eurail ticket for people who aren't European citizens or residents so if you're coming from Canada or South Africa or Japan, you'll need to buy that instead. It's pretty much the same thing though.

Rail apps and train reservations

Rail Planner is the Interrail/Eurail app and you'll definitely need it if you have a mobile pass as it's here where you will find your mobile ticket.

Even if you have a paper one, the app is really useful for trip planning. You can put in where you are going to and when and it will show you trains and connections. You can adjust preferred connection times so if you would rather not have to sprint for a connection, or you want time for a relaxing lunch, you can factor that in. We found this invaluable in the early planning stages as you can see exactly how long and how many changes it will take you to get from A to B. It made us realise that, for instance, it would take too long to go from Budapest to Split, even though it doesn't look too far on a map, so we dropped that idea early on.

I've seen a lot of criticism about the app but we found it very accurate. One particularly helpful feature is that you can just key in where you want to go and hit "now" and it will show you the next train.

However it's also very useful to download individual apps from different countries as these can warn you of delays, cancellations etc. Most will also tell you which platform your train is departing from, which is great if you don't have long for a connection or can't find a screen display.

We used DB Navigator (Germany), SNCB (Belgium), OBB (Austria) and NS International (the Netherlands). On the DB app, you could also see how full a train is likely to be, which can help you decide whether to book a seat or get a different train.

The Rail Planner app will tell you if you need to book seat reservations, and how to do it. You can make most of these through the Interrail website but also directly through the train operators.

On some high speed trains, reservations are compulsory and the cost of this can really add up, especially if there are four of you, so it's worth checking first before firming your itinerary. We dropped our plan to visit Paris for this reason – France seems particularly expensive for this. It's up to you whether you book reservations on other trains. We did on some long-distance trains e.g. Salzburg to Budapest as it was a five-hour journey. For shorter trips or those where there were frequent trains, we didn't bother.

Reservations were typically a few euros each so if we had changed our minds and decided to get a different train, we wouldn't have lost much. We managed to find seats on every train (apart from the one out of Brussels to Ghent), though not always together.

I was really surprised at the number of passengers

who, on a packed train, decided their handbag deserved its own seat. And also surprised about how few people asked them to move them.

If you don't book and you sit in a seat that someone else has reserved, then you'll need to give it up with good grace if it's claimed. Don't be grumpy like one or two people we had to politely eject from ours!

If you want to get a night train, it's worth booking as far in advance as you can because couchettes often sell out at peak times. We booked ours four months ahead as it was key to our journey. It was partially refundable until we downloaded / printed the ticket.

Planning ahead (or winging it)

If there's something you really want to do on your travels – climb the Eiffel Tower or visit a particular museum for example – then it is worth booking ahead, especially if you are travelling at peak time.

Yes, it cuts out the spontaneity but it also means you won't miss potential highlights of your trip. We booked the Van Gogh museum several months ahead. If you do want to go somewhere at short notice, it's worth checking the website a couple of days before you want to go to see if there are any returns. The Van Gogh museum emailed us a week before our visit with information but also asking us to let them know if we weren't coming after all, so someone else could use the tickets.

At the Anne Frank house, also in Amsterdam, tickets are released once a week on the website for six weeks' time.

You also need to think about how far in advance you want to book your accommodation. Now that booking ahead is so easy, I wasn't convinced there'd be any decent quality and/ or reasonably priced rooms available at the last minute if we weren't very organised. I booked around February for our July trip, though I did make a couple of changes later on, for instance swapping Brussels for Ghent. Even this far in advance, some of the cheaper accommodation had sold out, especially in youth hostels. I kept an eye on prices to see if they came down (so I'd know for next time) but as our departure date neared, there was little budget accommodation left. I felt pretty vindicated.

I mostly used booking.com to book hotels, as it was easy to have everything in one app and there didn't seem much difference in price. If I was doing it again, I would probably book more of the places directly as I know this benefits them.

With most hotels, you can choose to pay up front with no refund (the cheapest way of doing it.) Others allow you to cancel for free up to the day you arrive, or sometimes up to a few days in advance. Paying so much up front made me nervous so we mostly chose the option where you could cancel up to three days beforehand. It meant we still had some leeway to change our minds or change our plans if something went wrong.

For Baden-Baden, we had to pay about two weeks in advance. There had been German rail strikes earlier in the year, with threats of more, so I was a bit worried about it and considered cancelling and choosing somewhere else. I wasn't convinced travel insurance would cough up if we couldn't get there, because I knew about the strikes before we travelled (though not before we booked). It was great value though so I decided to stick with it, which turned out to be the right decision.

I've talked a lot about planning and I should point out there is another way to interrail, popularly known as "winging it". Wingers have a vague plan, or no plan at all, and wake up in the morning and decide where they'd like to go today. Don't like a city? Leave early. Enjoying where you are? Stay an extra night.

If you take this approach, you book accommodation on the day or just a couple of nights ahead. This leaves you flexible in case of bad weather/ train strikes/ changes of mood etc. The interrail groups are full of wingers enjoying the spontaneity and sometimes being rather smug about it. I did notice, however, that these tended to be people travelling alone or with one other person, rather than a group of four like us, and that they were mostly travelling out of peak season.

On my past interrail adventures, I was a winger, with a route in mind which could and did change on a whim (like swapping Athens for Amsterdam as mentioned above).

But then I was young, not particularly bothered about where I slept, it was late September and I didn't have teenagers in tow. More to the point, because no-one had thought to invent the internet or email yet, hardly anyone booked in advance so there was much more last-minute accommodation available.

I couldn't help feeling disappointed when I realised we'd lose some of the freedom that I associated with interrailing by planning everything so much, but the boys were practical about it. They pointed out we'd spent hours (and hours and hours) deciding where we wanted to go and when so there was no need to wing it.

One thing you don't need to do is buy your interrail ticket ages in advance as they don't use dynamic pricing.

Hotels, hostels and apartments (and the importance of the washing machine)

Usually when we go on holiday, I spend ages finding the right hotel but now I had to choose about 10 different places to stay. I wanted to book a couple of nice places at various points as a treat, but we needed to be practical. We had to pay full price for the boys in most places and four adults for three weeks in Europe at peak season equals, well, a scary amount of money. We set a budget of about £160 a night, ideally including tourist tax. This was particularly challenging in Switzerland. I quickly gave up on Amsterdam as everywhere was so expensive and we stayed in Delft and Utrecht instead.

We decided that we were happy to share a room to cut down on costs but this did restrict us a little as not everywhere has quadruple or family rooms.

Location was particularly important. There were a few places where we were only going to spend one night so we really didn't want to waste time getting a bus to where we were staying. Here, as time was so precious, the most important thing was to find somewhere near the station so we could drop off bags and be exploring a few minutes after arriving. On Saturdays, of course, we needed to stay somewhere that was near or easy to get to a parkrun.

We knew that eating out would really bite into our budget so we wanted to be able to cook our own meals in a few places. About half the places we stayed at either included breakfast, or breakfast came at a very reasonable additional cost. We decided if we could get breakfast for under £5 a head, it was worth it – otherwise we would buy cereal or get pastries out.

I also had to find places where we could do our washing at weekly intervals as we were only planning to take small cases. I did stop to laugh at myself because checking whether your accommodation comes with a washing machine is just so incredibly dull. I'm pretty sure I didn't wash a single thing when we went interrailing before. I can't remember whether I packed more than 20 pairs of knickers or wore them all several times. It's probably best not to think about it.

I booked a couple of hostels, one private apartment, a budget hotel or two, a few family-run guest houses and some serviced apartments, constantly checking I had the date right and that I wasn't going to leave us double booked or under-booked. I read reviews carefully and kept an eye out for things that sneakily weren't mentioned, like air conditioning. I made sure we had air conditioning in Budapest, which I correctly assumed would be our hottest stop.

I originally thought we'd mostly stay in Airbnbs but if you are only there for a couple of nights it seems to be expensive as you have to pay a cleaning fee and service charge each time. We only stayed in one apartment and realised that we did like having a reception where we could ask advice on where to go and so on.

Of course another option is youth hostels, which we use quite a lot in the UK. If you are not familiar with these, you can book a bed in a dormitory but they also have private rooms. Some are en suite and some have shared bathrooms and many are similar to, or even better than, budget hotels. All youth hostels aren't alike though. Back in the UK we have come to rely on their self-catering kitchens but the two we stayed in on this trip didn't have this option.

We stayed at two youth hostels, for one night each, and had a private family room with an en suite bathroom in each case. In Utrecht, we stayed at the Stayokay hostel which I can really recommend. It was central, the staff were lovely and it had its own bar and restaurant. We were tired on our night there after a long journey so having a fabulous hot chocolate at "home" was wonderful. Another direct booking, this was our cheapest stop, though that included reductions for booking early and also for being YHA members at home.

I was worried that a couple of the places we booked would be very basic but reminded myself we were only really going to sleep and shower there so it didn't matter an awful lot. Far better to spend the budget on *doing things* once we were there.

One thing I hadn't really thought about was whether there would be staff on hand 24/7. If you have a tendency to lock yourself out or need to ask where you can find a chemist at 3am, these can be very handy. Two of ours – in Lausanne and, infamously in Delft when the fire alarm went off in the middle of the night

– had no overnight staff on duty so do check this if it is important to you. Also be careful to check permitted arrival times if, for instance, you are likely to arrive very late at night. The reception at our Lausanne hotel was also closed for a while in the middle of the day.

I was pleased to come across a few budget hotel chains I hadn't heard of before that seemed popular with reviewers. There's Adagio Access apartments where you can self-cater (in your own room, not a shared kitchen) so you don't have to fork out for meals unless you want to. We stayed at one of these in Ghent and it was one of our favourite places, probably because it was so shiny and new. I booked directly with this one – if you want to do the same, make sure you become a member. It's free to join but you get a discount when you book.

Another chain of budget hotels is Meininger, where you can stay in private rooms or dorms. It feels like a cross between a hotel and a youth hostel. They offer discounts if you have a child under 18 with you so it's a good option for families. Our Brussels one, again booked directly, was excellent with helpful, multilingual staff and good prices for Brussels. It was very near the station which was key for us given our early start. This one did have a self-catering kitchen.

We had two-bedroom apartments in two places – Baden-Baden, which was in a private block and the Escala Suites in Budapest which was a serviced apartment. If you haven't heard of these before, these are a cross between a hotel and an apartment. Rooms are cleaned and there's a reception. This one also included an excellent breakfast in the price.

Everywhere we went, we found staff helpful and courteous and more than happy to store luggage. Both youth hostels had a lockable luggage room where we could store our cases for free before our next train, as well as lockers which you had to pay for.

One final tip: most places where we stayed had some sort of city tax so it's worth checking if it is included or not (mostly it wasn't) and who has to pay it. Children are often exempt but the maximum age varies.

Money: cards and cash

How you pay abroad has changed so much over the last few years. Just a couple of years ago I'd be using a credit card and thinking myself lucky as it was so much easier than travellers' cheques were back in the day. However there was a transaction fee each time.

A few years ago I started using a currency card (mine is FairFX). You can buy currency whenever you want, so I would load it up when the pound was high against the euro. You then use it as a normal card abroad and there are no charges.

A year or so ago, I got a Chase card which doesn't

charge transaction fees and uses Mastercard's exchange rate. I mostly used this on this trip as it didn't matter what currency you paid in – and it would then instantly convert it to pounds on your statement. You can also get interest and cashback on this. Other cards I've heard good things about for use abroad include Revolut and Monzo.

We took about €100 in cash as well as £40 each in Swiss francs and Hungarian forint – you never know when you are going to need cash for toilets or small purchases. My biggest surprise was in Baden-Baden where not everywhere accepted cash – in fact it was the first thing they said to us in one café. We had to go to a cash point on the first day and after that carefully checked that restaurants where we ate dinner did take cards.

I'd expected to spend quite a lot on "doing things" – activities and entrance to museums, for example. Ultimately though, this cost a lot less than I thought, partly because I had under-estimated how much time we would spend just wandering about and getting the feel of a city. We paid most for activities in Budapest and Salzburg but the latter was reduced through judicious use of the Salzburg card.

I'd completely forgotten to get our boys student cards so I kicked myself the first time I saw a student rate. I assumed we'd have to pay full whack for them in most places, but whenever there was a student rate we just asked for that and were given it. Kit was only asked to prove it on the one occasion (when he showed his A level timetable). Rory got free admission to the Van Gogh museum as he was under 18. I don't think 16-year-olds get in free anywhere in the UK.

One thing I hadn't really anticipated was how much we'd spend on public transport. In Baden-Baden, we had to get the bus four times and it was over 11€ each time. As mentioned above, Budapest was good value, especially the group travel card. We also had to pay for the metro in Brussels at €2,40 a throw.

We also spent quite a lot on coffee and beer stops, which added immensely to the enjoyment of the holiday. Adrian always had the perfect place in mind when we stopped for cake, which drove us mad at the time but he had an unerring habit of finding it (and a tendency to be extremely smug about it). Between us, we got through a heck of a lot of apple strudel, milkshake and coffee.

Travelling with teens

We hadn't spent so much time together as a family since lockdown, so a three week trip was potentially a challenge. Overall, we got on pretty well, without too many squabbles.

I think that key to this was that everything about the holiday was democratic. The route was a joint decision and the boys had just as much say as we did. I showed them all the accommodation before we booked it and discussed the options with them. For instance, in Salzburg, the choice was between a slightly posher hotel further away or a cheaper one near the station. Because we wanted to pick the bus up from the station early on Saturday morning to get to parkrun, they decided on the latter.

Apart from a total of six nights in two-bedroom apartments, we were in a family room for reasons of economy. When my mother announced she would give us a contribution towards the holiday (thanks Mum!) I asked the boys if they would rather get a separate room in some places. They declined and said they would rather spend the money on "doing stuff".

The boys also used post-exam time to research what we could do at each of our stops, so it certainly wasn't a case of the adults deciding what we'd do when we got there. We'd never have known about the Illusion museum, for instance, if it wasn't for Rory. That turned out to be a real highlight.

We told the boys what the budget was which helped too. They appreciated that we couldn't eat out at gourmet restaurants every night or fill every single minute with activities.

The boys were a massive help overall. They sorted the glitching Rail Planner app and were a complete whizz with Google Maps so we rarely got lost. Kit expertly navigated us on the Black Forest walk (with a little bit of help from the signs!) They were both extremely good at working out the public transport too. Rory even managed a few words of German.

I thought we'd split up and do different things more than we did, but apart from my Sound of Music tour and the last days in Delft when the boys found parkrun/ failed to find anywhere to go kayaking, we pretty much stuck together.

While we hope to do another family interrail trip next year, Adrian and I are also dreaming of going on our own. We'll definitely miss the teens' tech skills though (and their witty conversation, obviously.)

Useful websites

- The Man in Seat Sixty-One (www. seat61.com) is a massive website devoted to train travel. There's a huge amount of information here about how to travel around Europe by train and it is a good starting point.

- Interrailing for the Older Crowd (Facebook group). Aimed at the more mature traveller, this is a really lively page and if you have any sort of question, you can almost guarantee someone will answer you – and quickly. For instance, before our trip I asked advice about whether we should spend a night in Cologne or Munich, and how long in advance we needed to make reservations. When we were in Brussels, I asked if anyone knew anywhere near the station where we could get pastries at 6am and got plenty of answers. I love this group for its inspiring trip reports, especially from older people doing their first interrail trip, or going back to it for the first time since they were twentysomethings. There was a (sadly probably one-off) half-price interrail ticket sale in 2022 to celebrate interrail's 50th birthday. Many people took advantage of that to get back on the rails. All through the trip I kept saying, "Well, according to Interrailing for the Older Crowd..." which made the kids groan a lot.

- Interrail & Eurail Travelers is another busy and helpful Facebook group. This one seems to be aimed more at younger people.

- Interrailing and Rail Holidays with Families is a smaller Facebook page for people travelling with kids.

- The official Interrail website is really useful especially in the early days when you are trying to work out which pass you need. There's all sorts of practical information here including how to download your mobile ticket and an "ask the community" section where you can ask questions. Again, you'll usually find people will get back to you here. You can also contact the support desk. I had a question and they replied to me pretty quickly.

- The parkrun tourism Facebook page is excellent if you want to do a parkrun (please do a parkrun, it's a great way to see a different part of a new city and meet locals and other tourists). You can ask questions here e.g. about how to get somewhere – we found out which bus we needed to get to Hellbrunn, for instance. For more specific information, each parkrun also has its own Facebook page. You'll be able to see pictures and get an idea of the route for each one. You can read plenty of comments here which might help you make your mind up about which one to do. Check the page in the morning of your run for any updates e.g. last minute cancellations due to the weather.

Twelve top tips for a successful interrailing holiday

1. If you're booking an attraction like a museum, be wise with timings. We thought that if we booked the Van Gogh museum for late afternoon, we'd spend the whole day looking at our watches and wondering if we had enough time to do something. Our strategy was to book it for first thing so afterwards our time was our own.

2. If there is something you desperately want to do somewhere, and it would ruin your holiday if you don't, check opening hours before you book your accommodation etc. Some museums may close on particular days, notably Mondays which can potentially be a problem if you're not there for long. Also check supermarket opening times if you are self-catering for the same reason.

3. Don't over-do it. Sometimes I look at people's itineraries on Facebook groups and shudder. There are no prizes for visiting the most countries. It can be a bit dissatisfying to spend less than 24 hours in one place, as we found particularly in Lausanne, and when we go interrailing again, I will cut out the one-night stopovers. Some people advise a minimum of

three nights in each stop which is a good rule of thumb but even so that doesn't take into account travelling time. If you spend three nights in a city but don't arrive until the evening, you've lost a day there. Take this into account when planning your route. Also, allow time for beer and coffee stops to refuel and people-watch.

4. Download the rail planner app as soon as you start to plan your trip. It will show you how long it will actually take you to get a train from A to B.

5. Download the apps for the national train operator of whichever country you are in. This can be useful to allow you to check delays, platforms etc.

6. Avoid staying in big cities, especially if you have a continuous pass so you don't have to pay extra for the commute. It's cheaper and more relaxing.

7. Book key journeys like Eurostar and any sleeper trains early in case they sell out.

8. When your journey involves changing trains, be realistic with connecting times. A five minute connection doesn't give you much leeway for trains to be late, or to find your platform, and is stressful. In the Rail Planner app, you can change the default transfer time to various times including at least 30 minutes, or two hours etc.

9. Every interrailer knows to take comfortable shoes – but also think about comfortable socks. My massive blister was caused by some cheap trainer socks I'd bought. When I switched to the running socks I'd brought for parkrun, my feet were much more comfortable.

10. If you're in a group, share things like routes and hotel addresses somewhere that everyone can access – just in case your phone runs out of battery / gets lost at the critical moment. We created a special family interrail WhatsApp group for this.

11. Never give up an opportunity to use a free toilet! You have to pay for them in many cities and you may need coins which you won't necessarily have. Whenever we stopped for a coffee or went to a museum, we'd use the loo before we left. Also take advantage of toilets on trains, rather than at stations, which again you may have to pay for.

12. Take a teenager! Ours were incredibly resourceful and came up with great ideas of things they wanted to do. Also, they were much better with Google Maps than either of us. They do eat a lot though!

Acknowledgments

Cover illustration by Sandra Staufer
www.sandrastaufer.com

About the Author

Judy Yorke is a journalist, editor and writing trainer, who has worked for national magazines and newspapers for more than 30 years.

After the blog she wrote during her interrail trip gained a cult following, someone said she should write a book. For once, Judy did as she was told, and *Crowded Platforms and Window Seats* is the result.

She lives in Brighton with her husband and two sons.